VW BUS

THE FIRST 50 YEARS 1949–1999

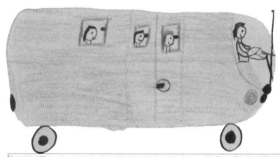

This summer we traveled by car. We went far away from home. Our car is different than any other car. It is bigger. It has three seats.

Yours has two seats. We have a Volkswagan bus. Your car skips over bumps. but our car gos right over the bumps. I like to sit on the motor. You see that our moter is in the back of the car. My dad says when you sit in the front of the car it looks like a airplane going off the ground. We can put 11 people in our car.

We love our car. Our car is green and white. We can see everything. When we go away for the summer we can bring any thing. Our car is funny because it has three doors on one side and one door on the other side. We can take the seats out. And we can turn the seats around and put a table in the car so we can play games.

Lydia Gross

VW BUS

THE FIRST 50 YEARS 1949–1999

BY KEITH SEUME

WITH MICHAEL STEINKE

BAY
VIEW
BOOKS
FROM

MBI Publishing Company

To Heinz Nordhoff and Ben Pon,
without whom there would be no story to tell

First published in 1999 by MBI Publishing Company, 729 Prospect Avenue,
PO Box 1, Osceola, WI 54020-0001 USA

© MBI Publishing Company, 1999

MBI Publishing Company books are also available at discounts in bulk
quantity for industrial or sales-promotional use. For details write to
Special Sales Manager at Motorbooks International Wholesalers &
Distributors, 729 Prospect Avenue, PO Box 1, Osceola, WI
54020-0001 USA.

Library of Congress Cataloging-in-Publication Data Available

ISBN 1-901432-26-2

On the front cover: Colourful and evocative artwork of a split-screen Samba
from a 1959/60 Volkswagen brochure, by an unknown artist.

On the half-title page: A classroom essay by Lydia Gross of Pennsylvania,
extolling the virtues of her father's Volkswagen bus. It was published in
Volkswagen of America's *Weathervane* newsletter in April 1965.

On the title page: A busy late 1950s street scene, again by an unknown
artist, shows most of the split-screen range, including Samba, panel van,
pick-up and Kombi.

On the back cover: This carousel of models, with canopy slogans in various
languages, is a very collectable piece of Volkswagen memorabilia.

Edited by Mark Hughes
Designed by Bruce Aiken

Printed in Hong Kong

CONTENTS

INTRODUCTION

Has there ever been a better loved or more universally praised commercial vehicle than the Volkswagen Transporter? Somehow, I doubt it. In all its forms, from the utilitarian delivery vans to the best-equipped campers, the Volkswagen Type 2 (to use the correct terminology) has won over more hearts than any similar vehicle.

When it was first launched late in 1949, the Transporter was showered with praise by all who drove it – even the often sceptical motoring press saw that this was something rather special and published glowing reports about this most amazing vehicle. At a time when rival manufacturers could only build crude, slow, unreliable vans, Volkswagen proved that the dependability of its world-beating Beetle was no flash in the pan – buy a VW and you could wave goodbye to roadside breakdowns and high running costs.

Throughout the 1950s, the Transporter was the subject of a never-ending development programme which saw the range grow to include ambulances, fire trucks, single-and double-cab pick-ups, mobile shops, ladder trucks, campers and far, far more. They were also converted, by several independent companies, into all manner of strange vehicles, including a half-track for use in mud and snow and a rail-car that ran on German railways. How's that for versatility?

When Volkswagen eventually dropped the original Split-screen model in favour of the all-new second generation 'Bay-window', the tradition continued, with this latest design being greeted with equal affection and respect. Even when the third-generation Transporters were launched in 1979, it was obvious that Volkswagen was still capable of producing a world-beater. But the story doesn't end there, for the legendary reliability and ruggedness can still be found in the later T4 and LT models, while the modern-day Sharan is perhaps the ultimate expression of a Volkswagen Microbus.

This book serves as a celebration of 50 years – sorry, the FIRST 50 years – of the world's best-loved transporter. It is not a definitive history, or a restorer's guide, but a largely pictorial acknowledgement of the important role which this trusty vehicle has played in the second half of the 20th Century. Consider it a family album, full of snapshots of a familiar friend at work and play throughout the world. I hope you will enjoy the photographs that we have unearthed, the vast majority of which have never been published anywhere before.

With this in mind, I must take this opportunity to pass on my heartfelt thanks to two people who have become great friends. First, Michael Steinke in Frankfurt, Germany, whose knowledge of Type 2 history knows no bounds. His Classic Volkswagen Transporter Archive (or 'Bulli-Archives'), with its priceless collection of Volkswagen promotional material, is second to none and the fact that he was prepared to share so much of this with us is a true measure of his devotion to spreading the Transporter gospel. Without Michael's help, this book would not have been complete.

And then I must thank Eckberth von Witzleben, archivist at the Volkswagen Museum in Wolfsburg. Eckberth has offered unlimited access to the most treasured of material, much of which has not seen the light of day for almost 50 years, and clearly enjoyed helping to unearth many of the treasures that appear on the pages which follow.

I would also like to thank 'Uncle' Jerry Jess in Arizona for his help in unearthing many amusing and fascinating photographs of some of the more weird and wonderful things that people get up to with their buses; the staff of *VolksWorld* magazine for the use of some photographs; and Martin Murray of Eirespares, Tipperary, for allowing me to borrow his rare photos of the signwritten vans from Ireland. Also, thanks to Ulf Kaijser in Sweden,

Finally, I would also like to thank my wife Gwynn for her help and support, especially while trawling through the Volkswagen archives, and editor Mark Hughes for his assistance.

If I have any regrets, it is that there is not enough space to publish all the photographs which have come my way over the last few months. Although we have used not far short of 500 photographs in the book, there are almost as many again which we could not find room for. Perhaps we shall have to wait until we celebrate the Transporter's centenary to show you those. Until then, enjoy the images as we look back over half a century of the Volkswagen Transporter.
—Keith Seume

CREATING THE LEGEND
From prototype to world-beater

Has there ever been a better-loved commercial vehicle (or camper, or ambulance, or pick-up, or…) than the original Volkswagen Transporter? Somehow that seems doubtful. It's the most versatile, the most universally recognised, the most reliable and the most 'friendly' of all workhorses – and its story is fascinating.

Traditionally, its history is traced back to April 1947 when Ben Pon, the far-sighted Dutch Volkswagen importer, sketched out his idea of a VW-based commercial vehicle during a meeting with management at Minden in Germany. The story goes that Pon saw the 'mule' – a crude, Beetle-based load-carrier built under British Army occupation to carry heavy loads around the factory – and drew out an idea for a rear-engined, cab-forward delivery van. It's thus generally regarded that this was the initial inspiration for Volkswagen to design and build a Transporter.

However, from its pre-war beginnings, designs for the Beetle included ideas for a light delivery vehicle; at least one prototype was built immediately prior to the outbreak of World War II. Although the hostilities brought further

Above: From the very earliest days of the Volkswagen, a van version was considered. This conversion, based on a wartime Type 82 Kübelwagen, was intended for use by the German postal service.

development to a premature end, there were other VW delivery vehicles – and ambulances – which did see some form of limited production, many based on the military Type 82 *Kübelwagen*. Although these vehicles were very crude in execution, they served to show how versatile the Beetle could be and, at the same time, pointed the way forward for future designs.

Factory records, which are held in the archives at Wolfsburg, make one of the first official references to the Type 29 *Lieferwagen* (what we now know as the Type 2 Transporter) in a memorandum dated 11 November 1948, in which the head of the design department, Dr Haesner, asked for further staff to be appointed to his offices. Such was the enthusiasm for the project that it would be less than one year before the first prototypes would take to the road, and only a year and a day later (on 12 November 1949) that Heinz Nordhoff, head of

Volkswagen, showed the finished Transporter to the world's press.

There has been much discussion about how many prototypes were actually completed, and when. Although the records take some understanding, it now seems that three true prototypes were built, none of them issued with chassis numbers. The first was a panel van, built using a widened Beetle chassis, which proved to be far too weak and simply folded in the middle when heavily loaded. It was constructed in the experimental department at Wolfsburg and made available for road-testing on 11 March 1949. Finished in grey, with silver wheels, it had the engine number 1-0113088. Number 2 was the first to have a separate chassis, consisting of two longitudinal box sections and a number of structural outriggers to support the floor. The third was actually prototype number 1 rebuilt to incorporate the new chassis design. Numbers 2 and 3 were completed between April and June 1949.

A further series of five pre-production models, which included a Kombi (number 7) and a microbus (number 8), was built in the months up to November 1949; some of these vehicles were featured in the first brochure published at the end of the same year. Records then suggest that seven Transporters were built in January 1950, but it's possible that this figure includes those built at the end of 1949. In February, a further three were assembled, but none at all were completed in March. Why this apparent halt in production? Most likely it was because the assembly line was being readied for full-scale production, this theory being supported by the fact that no fewer than 309 units were built in April 1950, followed by 333 in May.

The first vehicle to be sold outside the factory was chassis number 14 – or, more accurately, 000014. This was delivered on 8 March 1950 to Autohaus Fleischhauer of Cologne and sold to a perfume company called '4711'. VW confirmed this fact in a news release marking the tenth anniversary of production, on 8 March 1960, and added that the previous 13 vehicles – all pre-production examples – had been retained by the factory for test purposes.

The first Transporter to be exported was supplied to Ben Pon, Amersfoort, Holland, on 17 July 1950 as an *Aufstellwagen*, or special display vehicle. It carried the chassis number 32 and was delivered finished in primer ready for repainting in the purchaser's own livery. This was subsequently resold to Knebel of Siegen. The first true export sale was to D'Ieteren of Brussels, the Belgian VW distributor; this was chassis number 724 and it was delivered on 8 June 1950.

The first Transporter to be sent overseas, chassis number 591, was delivered on 10 August 1950 to Volkswagen's own Brasmotor plant in Sao Paolo, Brazil, as a special display vehicle, for use at a motor show. It was what is known as a microbus – a window van with rear seating. The vehicle was subsequently resold to a customer in October that year.

Production continued at Wolfsburg until 1956, when it was transferred to a new assembly line at Hannover. From that point on,

there was no stopping the hard-working and versatile VW Transporter. Between 1949 and the first-generation model's final trip down the German assembly line in the summer of 1967, some 1,833,000 examples were built, although production of the familiar 'split-screen' VW buses continued in South America as late as 1975!

When the Transporter was officially launched in November 1949, with the first road test appearing in print that same month, it was showered with compliments by all who drove it. Rival vehicles were crude, slow, noisy and thoroughly uncomfortable by comparison and the press reports must have made their manufacturers squirm. However, it would take more than 15 years before anyone could offer a serious threat to VW's Transporter: Ford's new Transit, launched in 1966, was the vehicle that finally set alarm bells ringing in Hannover.

The Transporter began life powered by the Beetle's 1131cc engine, which produced a modest 25bhp. Although the front axle assembly was unique to the model, it followed the multi-leaf torsion bar design laid down by Doctor Porsche for his beloved People's Car. Similarly, at the rear torsion bars provided the springing medium, just as they did on the Beetle. The little saloon car also donated its transmission, a well-engineered, if slightly fragile, four-speed affair without – at least, to begin with – the benefit of synchromesh. That feature didn't appear until March 1953, and then only on the top three ratios. In fact, it was to be a further six years before an all-new, fully-synchronised transmission was fitted to the Transporter.

The original engine was upgraded to 1192cc and 30bhp in December 1953, this unit remaining in use on Transporter models until May 1959, when it was replaced by an improved design which still only offered the same power output – it was a further 13 months before the power rose to a heady 34bhp. The biggest advance came in January 1963 when a 1498cc engine, producing 42bhp, was offered to

American customers; Europe and the rest of the world had to wait until March for the chance to sample 'real' horsepower. Eventually, in October 1965, the trusty but rather feeble (for a well-laden commercial vehicle, that is) 34bhp 1200 was dropped from the range.

One interesting feature, incorporated partly to increase ground clearance and partly to improve performance by lowering the overall gear ratios, was the use of reduction gears at the ends of each rear axle assembly. These gears, first used on the wartime *Kübelwagen*, effectively reduced the final-drive ratio, giving the Transporter more sprightly performance at the expense of a reduced maximum speed capability. The only necessary change to the Beetle gearbox was to swap the crown-wheel assembly from one side to the other, as the reduction gears reversed the direction of axle rotation. Four reverse gears (and one forward!) would not have been a lot of use to customers.

Despite its modest mechanical specification compared with the turbocharged, fuel-injected 2-litre-plus engines fitted to today's delivery vehicles, the trusty air-cooled flat-four did a sterling job of powering Transporters to all four corners of the world. They may not have been the fastest vehicles on the road but, with the ability to cruise at around 55mph (more for the later 1500 models), they certainly weren't the slowest. Remember, in the '50s, most commercial vehicles were barely capable of reaching 55mph, let alone cruising at such a speed!

One mystery it appears we will never solve is who was responsible for the styling of the original Type 2. Ben Pon is credited with the mechanical layout and Heinz Nordhoff certainly had influence regarding detail changes in appearance, but no single person appears to be cited in company records as being responsible for the distinctive smiling face of the first-generation Transporters. That's a shame, for can there ever have been a more stylish commercial vehicle?

Even the Beetle didn't escape the attentions of the experimental workshop at Wolfsburg. This rather unusual conversion was designed to be used as an ambulance, with the stretcher poking through to the driver's compartment.

While the British Army was in charge of the Volkswagen factory at Wolfsburg immediately after the war, this crude VW-based transporter – little more than a mobile platform – was used to carry parts around the works. It is considered by many to be the forerunner of the Transporter.

After visits to Wolfsburg in 1946 and early 1947, Dutch VW agent Ben Pon spotted the factory's crude transporter and, during a meeting with VW's Major Ivan Hirst at Minden, scribbled out a design for a van to be based on Beetle mechanicals. The drawing survives to this day. Note the date: 23 April 1947.

By 1949, there were a number of prototypes running around the factory – this is number four of a series of 13 pre-production models. Note the lack of passenger windscreen wiper, the black-filled VW badge on the nose and the crude bodywork finish. Prototype number one had been built using a modified Beetle floorpan, but this proved to be too weak, collapsing in the middle when used to carry heavy loads.

This prototype was used in a number of early publicity photographs, sign-written with the legend 'Wolfsburger Delikatessen' (a play on words, suggesting the new Transporter was Wolfsburg's latest delicacy). Note that, in common with all early Transporters, it has no rain gutter above the windscreen and only a partial gutter along the sides. Licence plate reads 'Type 29' – the official works number for the project.

These two previously unpublished photographs were taken on 12 November 1949 at the official press launch of the Transporter. The first shows the press examining the new vehicles: a microbus in the foreground, a Kombi behind and a panel van at top right. In the other, Heinz Nordhoff is seen explaining a diagram of the new model to the press — note how similar it is to Ben Pon's original sketch from 1947.

From the beginning, two-tone paint schemes were considered. This prototype (left), number six or seven, shows how attractive the Transporter can look in something other than blue or grey.

An early prototype showing the wide double-doors. The rearward door is secured by simple bolts instead of a proper locking mechanism. Also worthy of note is the location of the front jacking point, which is behind the door pillar rather than directly under it. This design was later changed when it was realised that jacking up the vehicle at this point caused the body to flex badly.

An early publicity photograph (right) showing how spacious the driving compartment was. This appears to be prototype number four, judging from the photographic location. The forward siting of the handbrake necessitated a long stretch for the driver — a problem slightly improved in 1959 by moving the lever backwards but not fully addressed until the introduction of the bay-window model in 1967.

In November 1949, the very first road test of the new vehicle appeared in the magazine Auto LKW, Motorrad und Sport. The road test appeared to feature prototype number four, a heavily retouched photograph of which is seen at the bottom of the page. This is the same photograph issued by the factory and reproduced on the facing page of this book.

To begin with, early prototypes had the spare wheel mounted vertically alongside the engine and the fuel filler cap accessible from the exterior of the vehicle, alongside the engine lid.

The first time the Type 2 appeared on a magazine front cover was also in November 1949, when one of the other prototypes was photographed at the Wolfsburg factory.

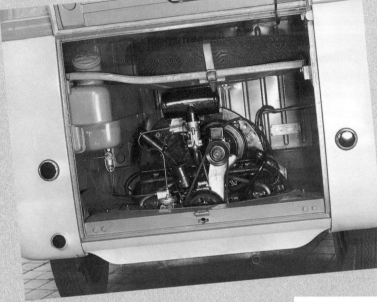

For production, the fuel filler was relocated, somewhat strangely, inside the engine bay. One would think that this was a recipe for disaster! The huge engine lid allowed excellent access.

At the end of October 1950, the spare wheel was moved to its new location above the engine. However, this particular photograph is of a vehicle built in April 1950, suggesting that it is was a prototype built to assess the new layout. Perhaps it was intended to be shown to Heinz Nordhoff for his approval.

The Transporter was a hit right from the start and the company's new-found optimism was reflected in the imagery portrayed in the contemporary brochures – this one dates from December 1950. The unique style of the artist, Bernd Reuters, perfectly captures the spirit of the era.

The Transporter relied on the basic 25bhp engine used in the Beetle saloon. The removable rear panel and large engine lid allowed the motor to be removed in minutes for ease of maintenance. This is prototype number six, which was featured in the first brochure of 1949.

Built on 16 August 1951, Loren Pearson's 'barn door' Transporter is one of the earliest in use today. Barn door models are so called because of the large rear engine lid.

Rare 1955 factory cut-away drawing of a pick-up shows the clever use of space beneath the pick-up bed. The fuel tank is located just ahead of the rear axle, while between that and the cab is a large storage locker. Note that, in March 1955, all Type 2s were equipped with a fresh-air ventilation system which drew in cool air above the windscreen.

Cut-away artwork of a 1955 Kombi model, the rear seats of which could be removed to increase storage space. On all van and bus models, the fuel tank was located above the rear axle. It's interesting to compare this illustration with Ben Pon's original 1947 sketch and note how little the concept had changed.

A rear bumper became standard on Deluxe models in March 1953, but remained optional on other versions for a further year. Starting handle could be called into use when the six-volt battery finally gave up the ghost on a cold day.

This cut-away illustration was used in the November 1953 brochure and shows the construction of the Type 2, with its substantial chassis and well-braced body. Note lack of rear bumper in this illustration.

1 Lenkgetriebe
2 Hauptbremszylinder
3 Vorderer Stoßdämpfer
4 Vorderachse
5 Entfrosterdüse
6 Federstablager
7 Radbremszylinder
8 Stirnrädervorgelege
9 Hinterachse
10 Getriebe
11 Kraftstoffhahn
12 Anlasser
13 Kraftstoffbehälter
14 Kraftstoffpumpe
15 Verteiler
16 Vergaser
17 Lichtmaschine
18 Batterie

One of a series of photographs taken in 1950 showing the Transporter on the assembly line at Wolfsburg (production was transferred to Hannover in the mid-'50s). Assembling these early models was extremely labour-intensive.

Conditions in the factory in the early '50s were a far cry from what you would expect to see in an assembly plant today. Much of the work was carried out by hand, including welding together major panels. Note the worker standing inside the engine bay!

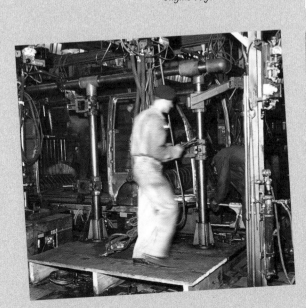

Separate body sections were assembled on a jig prior to welding. This photograph shows body sides being mated up to floor sections. What wouldn't a modern-day restorer give to have access to new panels like these?

Taken in 1953, this photograph shows part of the body assembly shop; bodyshells are lined up, having just come off the welding jig. Worthy of note is the right-hand drive (loading door on left) bus in the background on the right.

Once final welding had been carried out, a lot of time was spent finishing the bodywork by hand prior to painting. Here, a worker smoothes out the heat distortion caused by welding round the rear wheel arch of a pick-up.

With the fabrication stage completed, it was time for the bodyshells to begin their journey to the paintshop. They were transported by overhead crane using a large sling and cradle guided by the crane operator, seen sitting in the 'crow's nest' at top right.

The first stage in the paint process was a chemical dip to thoroughly cleanse the metal in preparation for priming. This was carried out using a tank large enough for the bodyshell to be dipped in one go.

The next step was to dip the body in a phosphate solution, which acted as an anti-oxidising agent. Could this be why so many early Transporters have survived to this day?

Prior to priming and the application of the final top coats, each bodyshell was painstakingly rubbed down by hand to ensure that it was perfectly smooth. It's hard to imagine how tedious this task must have been, day in, day out.

Even the roof came in for hand finishing but, due to the height of each vehicle, workers were forced to stand on steps to reach the top. Note the supply of running water to keep the paint surface lubricated during the rubbing-down process.

One of the few jobs which was automated, even as far back as 1956 when this photograph was taken, was the paint application. The bare bodyshells moved through the spray booth on a conveyor belt and paint was applied by swivelling spray nozzles.

Here, a worker drags a resin-loaded tack brush across the fresh paintwork to remove any overspray dust. Paint quality was exceptional, especially for a commercial vehicle.

Taken in 1962, the photograph shows workers preparing a Microbus for its two-tone paint finish. The bodies were masked by hand using paper and tape in readiness for a second trip through the paint booth.

Lines of 1962-model vans, pick-ups and buses await their turn as workers install the rear valances and bumpers. The pick-up on the far left appears to be still in primer finish, perhaps to special order to enable a customer to paint it in his own colours.

With the paint process completed, it was time to assemble the vehicles. This was carried out in a vast hall with every single operation carried out by hand. In the right foreground of this 1955 photograph is a Microbus fitted with rare 'Safari' windows – opening windscreens for use in hot climates.

A Samba (Deluxe) bus is fitted with its distinguishing side trim. To the right, a worker is getting ready to install the coloured plastic insert which was used in conjunction with the aluminium trim on Samba models.

Take your pick! A train-load of 1965 Transporters of all descriptions prepares to leave the Hannover factory for dealerships across the world. Loading gantry led straight from assembly hall to track side.

A very early vehicle shows the front bulkhead with its trim panel and dual passenger grab handles. Note that there is no trim panel on the seat frame, allowing a view of the large wing nuts which secure the seats to the floor.

A 1962 model awaiting delivery to the Deutsche Bundespost (German Post Office). The Bundespost has been one of Volkswagen's largest customers throughout the Transporter's life. It's curious that the vehicle shown has been equipped with US-specification all-red rear light lenses.

Various interior treatments were tried in the early days. This pre-Samba Kleinbus (small bus) features high-quality seat and door trim, along with dark-over-light two-tone paintwork. Note the grooved semaphore and location of jacking point – this is a late 1950 or early 1951 model.

Yet another variation on the theme, but this time there appears to be a storage locker under the rear seat and another behind it. Note the over-centre latch on the rear side window. This design was used throughout the life of the first-generation Transporter.

An extremely rare photograph of an even rarer vehicle: a double-door pre-Samba Kleinbus. Doors on both sides were very unusual, especially on a passenger bus of this vintage. Tilting seat backs facilitated access to rear seating.

A 1955-model Deluxe or Samba, officially called Sondermodell (special model type). This was the top-of-the-range model, with full-length sun-roof, roof windows and extra body trim, including chrome strips on the engine-cooling louvres and trim rings on the wheels.

The Kombi was an amazingly versatile vehicle, as this factory photograph of August 1963 is intended to show. At weekends, it could be used to transport the family, while during the week it could be transformed into a load-carrier by simply unbolting the rear seats.

A full-width dashboard was introduced in March 1955. Small gauge to the left of the speedometer (partly hidden by steering wheel) is a VDO fuel gauge, which was found on ambulances from the mid-1950s but not introduced for other models until 1961.

A modest celebration took place in the final assembly hall to mark the completion of the 10,000th Transporter-based ambulance built by the factory. The date is some time late in 1966; standing to the immediate right of the vehicle is Carl Hahn, the man tipped by many to succeed Heinz Nordhoff as head of Volkswagen — he achieved this in 1982.

Despite the rather amusing nature of this photograph, showing no fewer than 12 VW staff crammed into a multi-seater Kombi, it highlights a legal problem which beset Volkswagen in some markets. In many countries, the UK included, vehicles carrying more than eight persons were subject to a severe speed restriction, while in others the driver had to possess a special driver's licence. Volkswagen suggested its dealers tell customers that the Type 2 could carry just seven passengers (or eight in Germany post-1962), plus a driver.

The crew-cab was introduced as a regular model in November 1958, some six years after pick-up production began. Earlier, from the 'barndoor' period, it had been available to special order only. As a regular model it was first available with option code M16, but later received type number 265 (268 for right-hand drive).

High-roof models (option M222) – known in German as Grossraum-Kastenwagen ('big space van') – were popular with the fashion trade as they allowed dresses to be hung, full-length, from rails inside. This particular example was owned, however, by a brewery and used to deliver crates of beer.

High-roof models were produced by the factory to order and, other than their extended height, were identical to contemporary vans. This is a 1965 model which was restored in England by Mike Bailey, in the colours of the Feldschlößchen brewery.

This photograph shows the first shipment of VWs from Emden to the USA, on 10 March 1965. The cargo contained no fewer than 1125 Beetles and 225 Transporters.

The extra roof height made loading and unloading a lot easier, although the payload was no greater than that of a regular Transporter.

Due to the dusty conditions experienced in Australia, pick-ups were built with a special bulbous roof which incorporated air ducting to provide cooling to the engine. Ducts ran down the rear pillars of the cab and along under the vehicle to the engine bay. This allowed the factory to dispense with the conventional louvres stamped in the rear quarter panels.

Other odd variations on a well-tried theme were produced in South America, including this strange Microbus with two front-hinged side doors in place of the usual twin-door arrangement. Also worthy of note are the steps under the sill and front bumper, and the rear quarter windows.

By the mid-'60s, the VW Transporter was starting to lose its foothold in the marketplace to newcomers, such as Ford's new Transit delivery van. The Transit was the first of a new breed of small commercial vehicles which made VW's trusty 'bulli' look the 20-year-old design it was. As a stop-gap until the new 'bay-window' models came along, Volkswagen revamped the first-generation Type 2, with new door handles and a few other minor changes. However, the writing was clearly on the wall for this trusty friend.

'Safari windows' (option M132) were a popular option in hot climates and have become something of a 'badge of honour' among collectors, despite being prone to leaks. Their use necessitated folding windscreen wiper arms and a small plastic clip with which to hold them, known colloquially as a 'one-eyed duck' due to its shape.

Of all the 'split-screen' vans, among the rarest are those fitted with sliding side doors. Available as an option from May 1963, they gave customers a glimpse of the future, for the subsequent 1968-on models would come with sliding doors as standard. This particular vehicle, however, is literally doubly rare, for it's equipped with dual sliding doors (option M162). Owned by Type 2 restorer Alan Schofield, it's one of very few survivors.

A MOST VERSATILE MACHINE
The first-generation special-bodied models

No sooner had the Transporter gone into production than various companies began to investigate its suitability for a wide range of applications. One of the first was conversion into a mobile shop, complete with opening sales flap.

Volkswagen investigated such an idea as far back as 1951, barely a year after the Transporter had become available on the open market. At least one photograph exists of a prototype of such a vehicle, although it appears to be little more than a studio mock-up as there are no doors allowing access into the sales area! These first conversions were all based on the regular low-roof panel van, as the factory did not build a high-roof (*Grossraum-Kastenwagen*) model until late 1961. Spending a whole day inside a low-roof sales van must have been an unpleasant experience, a real recipe for a stiff neck! Fortunately, there were high-roof conversions available in the '50s, but they were the products of independent companies which did not have the factory's seal of approval.

When Volkswagen finally offered a high-roof van in 1961 there was no shortage of customers, among them Westfalia, long associated with the

marque as a producer of camper conversions. Westfalia's mobile shop was one of the most successful of all conversions, offering plenty of internal space for staff and goods alike, in addition to a well-thought-out sales desk and easily-opened side flap which offered protection against the elements.

There were other, rather more obscure, conversions based on the panel van, including bizarre mobile 'shop windows' with large glazed panels, behind which the owner could display his company's goods. Actually, this was quite a good idea, for the vehicle could still be put to use as a delivery van, despite the small loss of internal width due to the 'shop windows'.

Some of the most unusual conversions of all were the many hearses based on the Transporter, built by companies such as Christian Miesen or Frickinger. Some of these conversions were little more than panel vans

with large side windows cut into the rear bodywork, but others had true coachbuilt bodies, with gothic detailing, such as etched windows, coachlamps and flower racks.

In 1952, Volkswagen launched the pick-up, a versatile vehicle which soon won the affection of the construction industry. It was far more than a cut-down van, for it featured all-new bodywork from the cab doors back, including a large load area beneath which was a sizeable storage locker. With the optional canvas top (or tilt and bows, to give it the correct name) in place, the pick-up became an all-weather vehicle.

However, there was more for the pick-up to offer, but it took independent companies to come up with the ideas before Volkswagen itself put them into production. As far back as 1953, at least one company was offering a wide-body conversion, which allowed bulkier loads to be carried with ease. Such a vehicle didn't form part of the official line-up until 1957. A similar situation existed with the so-called crew-cab (or double-cab) – a pick-up with an extended cab which enabled up to six people to be carried, in addition to the open load. An independent company, Binz, first built a crew-cab back in 1953; this model is distinguishable by its rear-hinged ('suicide') rear door, which was noticeably longer than that used on the later factory-built crew-cabs. Volkswagen finally realised there was a demand and sold its own version from 1958.

The pick-up continued to come under scrutiny from all manner of users. In 1953, Meyer-Hagen, a specialist company which built fire trucks, marketed a VW pick-up complete with an extending ladder mounted on a substantial framework on the pick-up bed. A pair of wind-down steadying 'feet' ensured the vehicle wouldn't tip over when the ladder was fully extended. Such vehicles became the mainstay of provincial fire departments across Germany and neighbouring countries for over 25 years.

Although Volkswagen built the versatile Kombi and Microbus, each offering seating for seven or more passengers, there were several companies which produced their own variations on the theme. One of the most stylish was the Carlux built by Ernst Auwärter of Stuttgart, with panoramic roof windows to enable passengers to view the countryside with ease. Others were less attractive, such as the bus built by the East German Dresig company from parts salvaged from an ex-military *Kübelwagen*.

Such vehicles are, however, almost mundane by comparison with some conversions. Take, for example, the *Filmwagen Cinecar* or 'Kinobus', a mobile cinema designed to show training films at dealerships. What is believed to be the sole surviving example, now resident in America, is based on a high-roof panel van, with a fold-out screen in the rear and a complex projector unit inside what would normally be the load area.

Still not bizarre enough? Then how about the amazing Raupen Fuchs half-track conversion which appeared in the mid-'60s? This unlikely machine consisted of a VW Kombi adapted to run on tank-like tracks and was intended for use by forestry workers, ski resorts and farmers. One example still exists, forming part of the German Bulli Kartei's mobile display.

Strange through the half-track bus might seem, the prize for the most unlikely use of a Transporter has to go to the rail-car conversion, built in 1954 by Beilhack. Devoid of its regular wheels, rubber tyres and even its steering wheel, the Beilhack bus was adapted to run on railway tracks, having been fitted with the solid flanged steel wheels more normally seen on locomotives.

Dictionaries have it all wrong when they spell the word 'Transporter'. It should be spelled V-E-R-S-A-T-I-L-E...

The low-roof shop was a factory-approved conversion which was available to special order only. This view is from an original brochure dated 1962.

VW-Verkaufswagen (SO 1)

This brochure, from 1957, shows a conversion carried out by Westfalia. It is unusual in that it is a mobile shop based on a low-roof van, rather than the high-roof model. One can imagine that the person serving from this all day would end up with a rather stiff neck!

In 1962, Westfalia offered this high-roof shop (this is possibly the prototype) which was far more practical as a design than the low-roof version, allowing staff to stand upright while serving. It was eventually offered as a factory option (M221).

Westfalia wasn't the only company offering shop conversions, for this photograph shows a privately-converted high-roof model based on a late 1963 Transporter. Although similar to Westfalia's vehicle, it differs in several details, including the design of the hinges and stays.

Inside view of a Westfalia shop shows the lever arrangement which was pulled down to open up the side sales flap. It is based on a 'walk-through' van (the split front bulkhead allows direct access from the driver's compartment) and, in common with most mobile shop conversions, the double access doors are on the left side.

A very early mobile shop dating back to 1952 – note the ribbed bulkhead. It's uncertain how access was gained to the sales area as there don't appear to be doors! Possibly this is a photograph of a mock-up for publicity purposes only.

Another rare vehicle, this time a Westfalia shop with a small side opening which takes in the section normally occupied by the double side doors. The vehicle is a 1965 model.

Four Cities Imports, Inc in Alabama worked with the Southern Sash Co to build this mobile showroom in 1963. The display unit could be removed to allow the pick-up to be used as a delivery vehicle when necessary.

This is a one-off prototype mobile post office built jointly by Westfalia and Volkswagen to show to the Deutsche Bundespost. However, the DBP considered it too small and the project was abandoned. Stamp machines were concealed behind the rear door.

A row of Westfalia mobile display vehicles awaiting delivery. These were popular with many businesses as they could still be used as vans, yet allowed the display of the company's products.

Not every mobile shop conversion was carried out by a professional coachbuilding firm such as Westfalia. Many were home-brewed vehicles with simple box-like bodies built onto a regular Microbus or Kombi, such as this rather basic South American food stall.

Even less sophisticated is this home-made mobile shop built out of flat sheets of steel over a basic box-section frame. It may not be pretty but it gets the job done!

One of the most colourful vehicles based on a high-roof Transporter is this mobile 'American' hot dog van. The large sliding side windows allow access from either side, while the cooking equipment is located at the rear, above the engine.

American HOT DOGS

Pick-ups were very popular for local deliveries, especially with drinks companies. This early '50s pick-up was used by the Bielefeld-based Bluna soft drinks business to deliver lemonade.

The rear tailgate was replaced by a fixed display board which is, in turn, tied to the rear of the cab by the large 'Bluna' sign. The normal drop-sides remained in use.

Another variation on the drinks delivery truck theme was this pick-up used by Florida Boy orange juice. Unlike the Bluna vehicle, it did not retain the drop-sides.

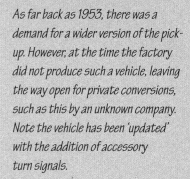

Westfalia carried out this wood-sided wide-body pick-up conversion, which gained factory approval and could be ordered through any Volkswagen dealership (option M201). The conversion was popular with builders and others who had to carry large loose loads.

As far back as 1953, there was a demand for a wider version of the pick-up. However, at the time the factory did not produce such a vehicle, leaving the way open for private conversions, such as this by an unknown company. Note the vehicle has been 'updated' with the addition of accessory turn signals.

This 1965 wide-body pick-up is still in use today and is equipped with a rare 'tilt and bows' (canvas top over a steel frame), which offers some weather protection to the open load. It's hard to find a workhorse like this in such good condition as most have led a hard life.

As early as 1953, the Meyer-Hagen company was offering this extending ladder conversion for the pick-up. It was primarily aimed at fire brigades but also appealed to tree surgeons and construction firms.

To enable heavy loads to be lifted easily onto the pick-up bed, Westfalia could supply this simple hydraulic crane, shown here fitted to a 1966 wide-body. Note the small 'foot' behind the front wheel to steady the vehicle while the crane is in use.

A full steel wide-body was eventually offered by the factory – this photograph dates back to 1958 but is in fact a 1959 model. While the drop-sides were the same as those used on the conventional pick-up, the tailgate was unique to the model.

So-called 'cherry pickers' were in widespread use by local authorities and electricity companies as they enabled maintenance workers to work on lamps and electricity cables without having to rely on a ladder. The striped legs on either side of the vehicle ensured that it did not tip over when the equipment was in use.

This fully-restored ladder truck shows how neat the conversion was. When folded away, the ladder rested over the top of the cab, while the steadying 'feet' were simply wound up or down depending whether or not the ladder was raised.

It's easy to see why this type of vehicle was so favoured by tree surgeons, for it enabled them to reach the tops of tall trees in relative safety compared to using a regular free-standing ladder. However, it still didn't offer a cure for vertigo . . .

What do you do when you need to carry a load that's too long to fit in the back of your pick-up truck? Why, you order this special trailer attachment allowing you to haul anything from scaffolding to telegraph poles. Normally you would remove the tailgate, so that the load could be carried without obscuring the rear lights.

Back in 1953, the coachbuilding firm of Binz decided there was a need for a new design of pick-up, one which could hold four people – five at a squeeze – and still be used to carry an open load. The result was this specially-produced crew-cab, which pre-dated the official factory-built version by almost five years.

What do you do when you have to carry a long load and four people? The answer is to use a crew-cab equipped with this trailer – at least that's what the Deutsche Bundespost decided back in 1961, when this photograph was taken.

Binz crew-cabs can easily be identified by their rear-hinged ('suicide') rear door which is also much longer than that fitted to the later factory version. Surviving examples of this ingenious conversion are scarce.

What are these people looking at? What's so interesting about the back of a Transporter?

What a way to go to school! This 1955 Kombi was used in the USA as a school bus and comes complete with roof-mounted boards and warning lights. The rear of the vehicle, in common with most American school buses, is painted yellow.

Ah, so that's what it's all about! This amazing mobile cinema could be used to show films at outside events, or maybe to show training films in workshops. The panel above the engine lid houses the loudspeakers. The projector and sound equipment are mounted just behind the cab divide and back-project the images onto the screen. As far as is known, this is the only surviving example of such a conversion; it now belongs to avid bus collector Charlie Hamill in the USA.

Just when you think you've seen it all, along comes another strange machine. This amazing railcar was built in 1954 by Beilhack. It used the regular Type 2 drivetrain but was equipped with solid steel wheels for use on the railway line.

This is the peculiar sight which greeted the driver: the normal Transporter instrument panel but no steering wheel! After all, with railway lines to follow, who needs to steer?

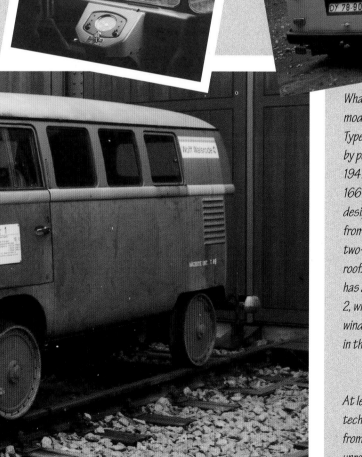

What at first appears to be a highly-modified Microbus is, in fact, not a Type 2 at all, but a one-off vehicle built by persons unknown using parts from a 1941 Type 82 Kübelwagen and a Type 166 Schwimmwagen! Many of the design cues have clearly been taken from the Transporter, including the two-piece windscreen and the peaked roof. From the rear, this unique vehicle has a look of the early 'barn door' Type 2, with its large engine lid and fixed rear window. Note the engine cooling louvres in the rear quarter panels.

At least one railcar survives, at the technical museum in Berlin. Apart from the wheels, it could be any other unrestored 'barn door' bus, but the railway track gives the game away!

Das Raupenfahrzeug für jeden Zweck und jedes schwierige Gelände wie Schnee, Sand, Wald und Wiese

Technische Daten:

Karosserie: Ganzstahl	Motor: 1482 cm³, 42 PS
Gewicht: 1300 kg	Getriebe: Autom. Sperr-differential
Lenkung: Zweiachsig	
Ladegewicht: 550 kg	Geschw. ca. 40 km
	Länge: 4280 mm
	Breite: 1980 mm

In answer to the shortage of new vehicles in the former East Germany, the coachbuilding firm of Dresig built this vehicle using parts from ex-Wehrmacht military VWs. Once again, its design is clearly influenced by the 'genuine article'.

No, your eyes don't deceive you – this really is a brochure for a half-track conversion on a Transporter! Offered in the mid-'60s by Raupen Fuchs ('Caterpillar Fox' in English), this unique machine was designed for use in snow, sand, forest and meadow, according to the brochure.

At least one example survives to this day (possibly the only one ever built?) and can be seen at displays staged by Bulli Kartei in Germany. Can you imagine the reaction of your local VW dealer if you took this in for a service?

Another very strange conversion was this one carried out by the coachbuilding firm of Ernst Auwärter in Stuttgart. Designed for use as a tourist bus, the 'Carlux' has a highly-glazed roof which allowed the occupants a better view of the countryside. The conversion was carried out by simply slicing off the roof at waist level and installing a new roof section.

Until recently VW fanatic Jerry Jess from Arizona was the proud owner of this hearse, which was converted by Frickinger in Germany. Also based on a pick-up, it features a less-rounded roofline than the Miesen conversion. The rear doors have no windows and carry Jerry's humorous 'Frankin Stein Mortuary' signwriting. 'Flotter Transport' lettering on the doors can be loosely translated as 'High Speed Transport'! All we can say is that the 'body' appears to be in perfect condition...

This is probably how any true VW enthusiast would like to take his (or her) last ride! Christian Miesen converted several Volkswagens over the years, many into ambulances. However, the most intriguing were the hearses, built using a pick-up as a base.

AT YOUR SERVICE

The Transporter in the role of life-saver

In the early '50s relatively few vehicles proved suitable for conversion for use by the emergency services. Most vans were crudely built, slow and quite agricultural in design – and they were frequently unreliable. With the arrival of the Transporter, however, fire and medical services across Germany sat up and took notice. Here, at last, was a vehicle which lent itself perfectly to use as a fire truck or small ambulance.

Many conversions were carried out by independent companies, who purchased new Transporters from Volkswagen and then rebuilt them to suit their new purpose. Meyer-Hagen was among the first to convert the Transporter into a vehicle for use by the fire brigade, the interior being extensively fitted out to accommodate not only hoses and tools, but also a fire pump that was powered by a Volkswagen engine. There were to be several variations on the fire truck, some designed to carry fire-fighting equipment as described, others – frequently Kombis – simply to provide transport for additional firemen or to carry tools.

However, mention the words 'fire truck' to most people and they will immediately think of a

Above: The first fire truck to be officially offered by Volkswagen appeared in this 1956 brochure. Prior to this, vehicles had been converted by independent companies.

traditional fire engine with ladder and turntable. Even Volkswagen got in on the act thanks to companies like Meyer-Hagen, Magirus and Bachert, each of whom equipped the VW pick-up with an extending ladder and turntable to allow it to be swivelled to one side or the other.

The first Volkswagen-based ambulance conversion was built in 1950 by Christian Miesen using a Kombi as a base. In 1951 the factory showed its own ambulance conversion, a prototype which, although based on the regular 'barn-door' Kombi, had a shortened engine lid to enable the inclusion of a separate tailgate (less rear window) to allow the stretcher(s) to be loaded from the rear. This pre-empted the post-March '55 redesign of the Transporter, with its tailgate and smaller engine access panel.

Many other ambulance conversions were in use during the '50s and '60s, including those by Westfalia and Clinomobil, the latter in the form of a high-roof conversion, which offered

considerably more headroom inside. There was also the fascinating 'Strahlenmesswagen' – an ambulance-like vehicle which carried monitoring equipment to check radiation levels in the event of a nuclear accident.

Not to be left out, the German Police also quickly adopted the Kombi for use as an emergency vehicle and many such conversions were, once again, carried out by Westfalia. However, not every Police department took up the DIN-approved Westfalia option, preferring to buy unmodified vehicles from Volkswagen and then seeking the services of a local workshop (or their own) to install the necessary extra lighting and other equipment.

What is truly amazing is how many of the original Split-screen emergency vehicles – primarily fire trucks and ambulances – are still in regular use. Often they were purchased by large companies for use on their own premises and saw relatively little service. Consequently, they never really needed to be replaced. Today, it's possible to find Split-screen fire trucks and ambulances still in service in the more remote areas of Germany, Switzerland and Italy.

This amazing cut-down Transporter was in use by the Volkswagen factory in the very early '50s, supplementing the large Mercedes fire trucks shown alongside. It's doubtful that this unique vehicle has survived.

The VW Museum at Wolfsburg houses this December 1952 fire vehicle which saw service until 1982, when it was allowed to retire gracefully. Worthy of note are the full-length roof rack and the single rear side window. The emergency blue lights are, sadly, not originally from 1952.

If it wasn't for the smiles on their faces, you'd think that this fire crew was on its way to an emergency! VW factory fire brigade put on a show for the photographers in 1959.

From the outside, the fire trucks looked like regular Transporters but inside they frequently carried a water pump powered by a Volkswagen engine. The pump unit could be slid in and out on rails.

Ziegler was one of the main manufacturers of VW-powered fire pumps. Water could either be sourced from a stand pipe, as shown here, or drawn from a nearby lake.

Magirus conversion on a single-cab pick-up features a 10-metre extending ladder. This rare photograph is of a 1964 model which had just been delivered to the Frankfurt fire department.

Kombis were also used by fire departments to transport extra firemen to the emergency. In this case, the fire pump and hoses were carried on a trailer.

High-roof fire trucks are not very common. This example was originally used in Switzerland.

Now in the Wolfsburg Museum, this single-cab fire-truck features a 12-metre ladder and was converted by Meyer-Hagen. This 1964 vehicle was in service until the late '80s!

Another conversion, this time by Bachert, featured a 10-metre ladder made of aluminium and steel, rather than wood. This particular vehicle was used as a company fire truck.

A Meyer-Hagen ladder conversion on a crew cab was not available from the factory; this 1962 example saw service in Italy until the '90s.

Not all fires can be put out using water – this Transporter is towing a trailer on which a dry-powder extinguisher system is mounted. This was for use on electrical and chemical fires.

This 1964 crew-cab is still in use with an Italian fire department and has covered just 8000kms since new! It's in immaculate condition and obviously well looked-after.

Members of Bulli Kartei put on a display of their fire vehicles. This German club has probably rescued more VW emergency vehicles than any other organisation.

A proud fire chief poses for the camera next to his 1964 double-door Kombi, which is also still in use in Italy. Note the wooden ladder and chrome-plated siren above the windscreen.

Many airports throughout the world used VW Transporters as emergency vehicles, and Frankfurt was no exception. Seen here in 1971, this 1966 example was a rare sliding side-door model. Note also the combined door mirror and spotlight.

Extremely rare photographs of a 1951 prototype ambulance built by Volkswagen. Note the roof vent and the tiny illuminated Red Cross sign above the windscreen. The interior view shows the spring-loaded step which popped out when the side doors were opened. The side-facing reclining patient's chair could be slid into the vehicle and locked in place. Note the frosted windows and protective 'jail bars'.

The rear of this 1951 prototype ambulance had been converted to accept a stretcher and, as a result, the engine lid now closely resembled that of the later (March 1955 onwards) models. However, at this time, the rear hatch was still hinged at the top.

Later ambulances – this is a 1959 model – had the rear hatch hinged at the bottom, to act as a support while the stretcher was loaded and unloaded.

Having already successfully converted Beetles into simple ambulances, Miesen turned its attention to the new Transporter in 1950 and offered its own conversion, which pre-empted that of the factory by a year.

Despite the utilitarian nature of such a vehicle, the March 1952 factory brochure for the ambulance was as stylish as any other VW publicity material of the time. Featuring Reuters' artwork, the cover illustration was accurate, right down to the petrol filler.

KRANKEN-TRANSPORTER

VW-KRANKENTRANSPORTER
„WERKSMODELL"

High-roof ambulance conversion was carried out by Clinomobil of Hannover on a 1967 model. Note the tow hook located just below the right-hand tail light.

The high-roof ambulance made life a lot easier for crew and patients alike, offering greatly increased headroom and plenty of storage space for equipment and medicines.

The rear hatch was in two pieces, the upper section hinging upwards, the lower downwards, as with a regular ambulance conversion.

A prototype ambulance conversion by Westfalia based on a larger box van. This offered much more space than the regular VW body design but is less than beautiful to the eye! Interior was much wider than normal. Rear doors hinged at the side, making them easier to open than one hinged at the bottom.

This 1952 ambulance featured a full-length roof rack, with cover, and a matching trailer. Loss of rear 'barn door' necessitated relocation of the fuel filler to the side of vehicle — note the D-shaped flap above the rear wheel.

A Westfalia ambulance (below) used by the Red Cross in Wiedenbrück, the company's home town. Interestingly it has not only a full-length 'Westy' roof rack and matching tent but also a full-length sun-roof!

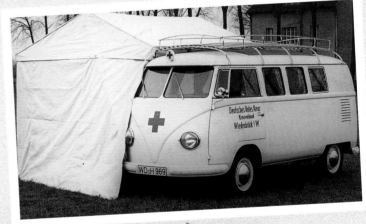

'For the people of Uganda . . . from the people of Germany', reads the signwriting on the sides of these 1962 ambulances. These versatile vehicles could be found in service throughout the world.

An unusual emergency vehicle in that it is based on a 1962 Samba (Deluxe bus), complete with specially shortened sun-roof to accommodate a radio aerial on the roof. It was originally used as a radio communications vehicle by the Bayerischer Rundfunk (Bavarian Broadcasting Co).

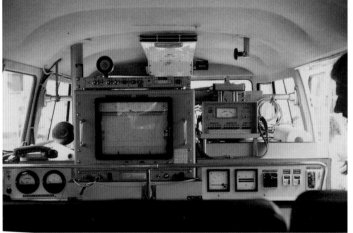

This may look like a normal ambulance (above and left), but its intentions were somewhat more sinister. This 'Strahlenmess-wagen' was built to measure radiation levels in the event of a nuclear catastrophe. Inside the equipment resembles something out of an old James Bond movie, but its intended usage reflected the concerns of a country caught in the middle of the Cold War.

Most ambulances were finished in ivory but this example was painted grey, the traditional colour for Red Cross vehicles in Germany until the late 1950s. Note the usual ambulance lack of rear window.

Westfalia sought to gain DIN (Deutsche Industrie Norm) recognition for its Police vehicles and this was duly granted. DIN approval meant that the vehicles met official standards required by Police forces across Germany. Note the special Police roof rack.

This Police Kombi was in use in Lower Saxony in the late '50s. It features a blue emergency light made by Auer and a forward-facing loudspeaker unit.

Westfalia conversion for the Police (above), but this time on a 1965 model with optional sliding side door. Note that, once the door is open, the ladder can be slid from under the roof rack to locate on the sill.

Not all Police forces purchased Westfalias — some opted to buy a basic Kombi (left) and have the vehicle modified locally. This is one such conversion, and is noteworthy for the unusual location of the warning lamp on the side of the roof.

Speeding motorists beware! This German conversion was produced for the Police and incorporated radar equipment front and rear to measure the speed of passing vehicles. Note the repositioned front turn signals.

Roof-mounted ciné projection equipment and loudspeaker are features of this Police Microbus used for road safety education.

The Dutch Police also used the Kombi to good effect. The photographer is standing on a purpose-built roof rack, ahead of which is a small siren.

THE SECOND GENERATION
The arrival of the Bay-window bus

The Split-screen Transporter had been in production for almost 18 years and had reached the end of the road as far as further development was concerned. The final nail in its coffin was the release of Ford's new Transit range in 1966 which, although thoroughly conventional in its drivetrain layout, offered more space, a higher level of equipment and vastly superior performance.

For dyed-in-the-wool purists, it was a black day when the much-loved Split-screen Transporter took its final trip down the assembly line to make way for the new and, it must be said, much-improved Bay-window models. The first-generation bus had been treated with so much affection by owners since the early '50s that, when its replacement arrived in August 1967, its demise was generally regarded as the end of an era. Surely no vehicle could ever prove to be so versatile or successful?

However, despite initial scepticism from enthusiasts, the new Transporter proved to be every bit as versatile as its predecessor and considerably more successful. After all, who can argue against sales figures of over 2.5 million,

Above: This pick-up was used by Volkswagen in the grounds of the factory. The 'WOB' licence plate denotes Wolfsburg while the small stencilled number above the bumper shows it to be a factory vehicle.

compared with just 1.8 million for the original?

Volkswagen's second-generation Transporter had several features which set it apart from the old model, not the least of which was the large, panoramic windscreen which helped to give the cab a bright and airy feel. Drivers also appreciated the new dashboard, with its full-width padding and easy-to-read instrumentation. The cargo area was increased in volume, while the standard sliding side door – previously an extra-cost option – made it far easier to load and unload bulky items.

But the redesign was far more than skin deep, for the rear suspension, formerly swing-axle with reduction boxes on each axle, was now a more sophisticated four-joint design, with two constant-velocity joints per axle. This had the great advantage of allowing plenty of suspension movement without any serious change in camber angles, with better handling as a result. It was

also to prove far more reliable than the earlier system and virtually maintenance-free. Later, in 1971, the braking system was improved, with the addition of disc front brakes.

The new Transporter also benefited from an upgraded engine, now of 1584cc, which produced 47bhp at 4000rpm. Later, in August 1970, the Transporter engines received cylinder heads with new dual inlet ports, which helped to improve performance still further by boosting power output to 50bhp. However, the best news was still to come when, in August 1971, Volkswagen offered a new 1679cc engine producing 66bhp, first seen in the Type 4 saloon car range.

This new engine was a revelation, even if history was to prove that it was never quite as reliable or easy to maintain as the original Beetle-derived unit. Later still, capacity and power increased to 1795cc (68bhp) in August 1973 and then to 1970cc (70bhp) in August 1975. This latter engine finally gave the hard-working Transporter the power it needed, although the original 1600cc motor was still available to those who preferred to take life in the slow lane.

One of the first publicity photographs announcing the new second-generation Transporter shows a right-hand drive pick-up and matching Transporter. The new look was a revelation, turning what was basically a 20-year-old concept into something modern and up to date.

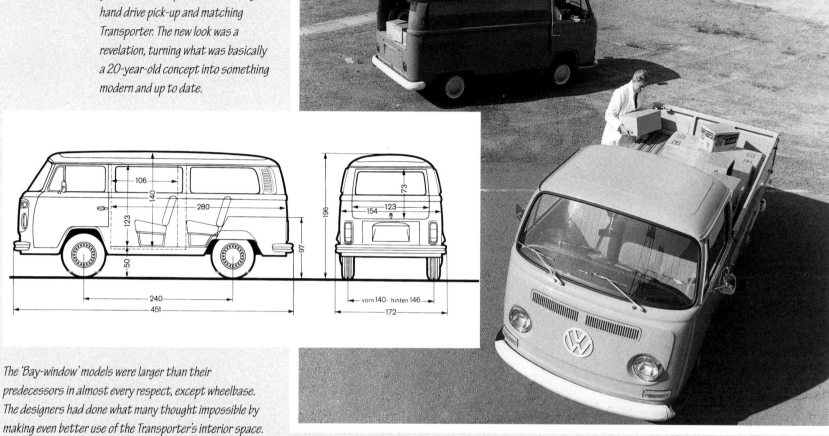

The 'Bay-window' models were larger than their predecessors in almost every respect, except wheelbase. The designers had done what many thought impossible by making even better use of the Transporter's interior space.

An unusual view of a pre-production model clearly shows the substantial chassis and outriggers, the latter adding support to the floor. The tube running along the centre of the vehicle is the heating duct.

One of the biggest technical changes made to the new-generation vehicles was the redesign of the rear suspension. This saw the demise of the old swing-axle system, replaced by a 'four-joint' design with semi-trailing arms. Torsion bars, however, still acted as the springing medium.

Much of the final body finishing was still carried out by hand, as this photograph shows. Build quality was exceptionally high for a commercial vehicle, one reason why so many have survived.

Once final assembly had taken place the bodies were hand-finished – welds were ground smooth and surface imperfections removed. The last task before painting was to go over the body, inch by inch, to remove any dust particles with a tack brush.

Volkswagen always prided itself on its inspection procedure, which weeded out the merely good from the perfect. Here a paint inspector examines a military-specification Kombi (note the fittings above the windows to allow the use of black-out blinds).

Once the paint process had been completed, it was time to rub down the paintwork by hand to give it its legendary VW shine. This photo, taken in 1967, shows one of the first of the new-generation vehicles to go down the assembly line.

Workers were understandably proud of their workmanship and were only too happy to be photographed alongside their products. This picture was taken in 1976 and shows a body ready to go to the assembly hall.

Bay-windows were assembled at Hannover on a dedicated assembly line. Although this photograph was taken in 1973, body assembly was still very labour-intensive. Note the 'Mole' grips being used to hold two panels together while the worker carries out the welding!

On certain of the assembly lines, the vehicles were moved sideways along a conveyor belt to enable workers to install the bumpers and rear valances. By this stage, the vehicles could be driven to the next stage of the assembly process.

A Kombi having its interior installed. This continued to be a popular model due to its amazing versatility. Note that Hannover also produced Beetles; the new 1968 models can be seen in the background.

It is interesting to note how many different types of vehicle shared the same assembly line. Here Deluxe buses can be seen alongside vans, pick-ups and even a military specification Kombi (the dull grey vehicle at centre left).

Rare Bay-window crew-cab reaches the end of the line. Second vehicle in the line has mountings on the door for extended mirrors, suggesting it is destined to be a Westfalia wide-body conversion.

Volkswagen normally painted commercial vehicles in blue or grey but, starting in the mid-'70s, bright 'safety' colours became popular, with orange being the favourite. Note the silver painted hubcaps – a small exercise in cost cutting.

The last task before shipping was to wax-coat the completed vehicles. This protected the paintwork and underside during shipping.

The full range of factory-produced Bay-windows, showing what a great line-up VW had at this time. The crew-cab remains a relative rarity, with the van and single-cab pick-up being the industry favourites.

Cheat! This particular photograph, taken late in 1967, is meant to show a right-hand drive model for the UK market, but is really a left-hooker. The photo was 'flipped' by the factory's printer — the giveaway is the fuel filler, which should be on the right side!

Crew-cabs are rarely seen and, for some reason, second-generation ones seem harder to find than their predecessors. Tilt and bows were useful accessories if you wished to protect the load area.

High-pressure headlamp washers were designed for Police use but were offered as an option to the general public. They are, however, extremely rare.

A prototype Microbus, pictured in 1973, showing new side trim and an alternative window arrangement. Generally, second-generation buses came with just one opening vent window per side.

In 1972, Volkswagen offered Transporter customers the new 1700cc air-cooled engine from the Type 4 saloon range. The new engine had much improved torque and power output over the Beetle-based 1600cc unit. It would later increase in size to 1800cc and, finally, a full 2 litres.

Volkswagen developed a battery-powered Type 2, largely for use in urban environments, and offered it for sale to the public. However, the biggest drawback, as with all electric vehicles, was a limited range and reduced payload. In fact, the batteries weighed almost as much as the recommended carrying capacity and the vehicles had to be fitted with heavy-duty suspension. The motor bolted up to the regular transmission and used the same mounting points as the petrol engine. Changing the battery pack involved a 'cartridge' system — the new batteries were slid in from one side as the old spent ones were pushed out the other.

Very few of the electric conversions were sold and even this is a mocked-up photograph. The 'WOB' licence plate and stencilled factory code numbers show this to be a VW factory-owned vehicle.

The later second-generation Transporters were a huge hit in the USA, where customers appreciated the improved performance offered by the new engine. American tastes dictated that extra trim be fitted, in this case round the windscreen and along the waistline. Chrome-plated mirrors were fitted to many US export models.

Another factory-based prototype: the Microbus was never sold without either opening vent windows or sliding windows in the rear.

Volkswagen do Brasil built a range of Bay-window vehicles which differed in several ways from their European equivalents. Note the three side doors, rear quarter windows and the domed hubcaps on this 1975 model. These South American Transporters can be considered something of a cross-over between the first and second generations.

SPECIAL TREATMENT
The new model is put to many uses

The new generation of Transporter soon became the subject of numerous official and unofficial conversions, ranging in style from the thoroughly practical to the decidedly unusual. In fact, it simply followed in the footsteps of its predecessor by displaying versatility unparalleled by any other vehicle.

One of the first special versions to appear was the factory-approved wide-body conversion built by Westfalia on the single-cab pick-up. This was aimed squarely at the construction industry, its large load-carrying area being perfect for the builder who needed to carry sand, bricks and other such loose materials. However, Westfalia wasn't the only firm to produce such a vehicle, for other companies could build similar conversions to order.

In response to customer demands, and following on from the wide-body pick-up, Volkswagen decided to build a tilt-bed conversion ('Kipper' in German parlance), again based on the regular single-cab model. This featured a hydraulic ram, the workings of which were located in the under-bed storage locker.

As was the case with the original

Above: 'We drive without petrol' says the slogan on the side of this '78 model Transporter. Used by the Rhein-Main airport, the van was battery-powered.

Transporter family, these variations on the pick-up theme were followed by a factory-built high-roof van conversion and several unauthorised models, all of which were popular with the fashion industry as the increased roof height allowed long dresses to be carried.

During the late '60s and early '70s, much thought was given to finding alternative power sources to the conventional internal combustion engine in an attempt to reduce levels of pollution, especially in urban areas. Electric power was an obvious choice and Volkswagen spent a lot of time and effort building battery-powered vehicles, but the most adventurous project it undertook was a gas turbine Bay-window Microbus. Sadly, this thoroughly unconventional vehicle, with its futuristic powerplant mounted in place of the usual air-cooled 'flat-four', never made it past the prototype stage.

Alternative drivetrains were also investigated, the most exciting of which was a

four-wheel-drive system which turned the Transporter into a very capable off-road machine. This project was the brainchild of Henning Duckstein, who worked at Volkswagen and, it seems, spent many of his vacations in North Africa. Duckstein's enthusiasm led to a small series of prototype vehicles being built, although an all-wheel-drive Bay-window never saw full-scale production. However, the project laid the foundations for the Syncro – the four-wheel-drive version of the third-generation Transporter which was to follow.

The accolade for the ultimate in alternative drivetrains, though, must go to a strange Bay-window model built in Indonesia, a photograph of which can be seen in this chapter. At first sight it would appear to be a regular VW Kombi but closer examination reveals a solid rear axle assembly and front-wheel-drive! This (presumably) one-off vehicle was built on the chassis of a VW 'Muli', a basic commercial chassis powered by a front-mounted air-cooled Transporter engine and developed for use in Third World markets.

An escort vehicle in use at Rhein-Main airport. Used to lead aircraft along the taxiways, this type of vehicle commonly had chequered paintwork. Large board at rear of roof bears the words 'Follow Me' on the reverse.

Volkswagen produced this limited edition, known as either the 'Silver Fish' or the 'Silver Bird'. It was introduced early in 1978, dropped from the range and then revived at the end of the same year.

A number of high-roof conversions were produced by different companies; most simply installed a glass-fibre moulded roof on top of the existing vehicle. This official factory conversion, however, included a unique side door, with extended top.

Wide-body conversion (above) was built for Volkswagen by Westfalia, using wooden drop-sides. This example has an after-market tilt and bows, something never offered by the factory for this model.

Tilt-bed pick-up (top right) was a factory conversion using a single hydraulic ram. The conversion, aimed at the construction industry, retains the original drop-sides.

An interesting view (right) of a wide-body pick-up. With the tailgate open we can see the special step and aluminium floor to the pick-up bed.

The Deutsche Bundespost continued to use the Transporter when the second generation was introduced late in 1967. Note the fittings for a padlock on the sliding door – an inexpensive security device!

Wild and whacky open-top bus was built for use on a TV show in Germany. Following its retirement, it was put to a new purpose at Wolfsburg to give visitors guided tours of the factory. It now resides in the VW Museum.

One of small run of prototype all-wheel-drive vehicles used to test the drivetrain for what would become the Syncro range of third-generation Transporters. The design was the brainchild of Henning Duckstein, a VW employee who, the story goes, spent most of his vacations in North Africa. He built his own prototype, which aroused the interest of VW engineers — and the rest, as they say, is history.

For the ultimate in alternative power sources, how about a gas turbine? In common with so many other turbine-powered prototypes, it never quite lived up to expectations. It was built in 1979 but was based on a 1973 model.

The ultimate in oddball second-generation Type 2s, this Indonesian-built vehicle is, in fact, front-engined, with front-wheel drive. It's based on the drivetrain of a 'Muli' — a simple vehicle developed by VW for sale in CKD (completely knocked down) form in the developing world. Note the small side-hinged rear door and heavily contoured side-panels.

EMERGENCY!
Bay-windows to the rescue!

As the first-generation Transporters were so popular with the emergency services (fire, ambulance and police), it came as no great surprise that the same authorities should, on the whole, embrace the second-generation models with equal enthusiasm. Indeed, the Bay-window vehicles had the potential to be even more successful in such roles for the simple reason that they offered greater interior space and improved performance. Low operating costs were another major factor, but, there again, why change your fleet of vehicles if there is nothing wrong with them? The Split-screen Transporters were indeed a hard act to follow.

However, with the advent of the 1.7-litre engines, followed by the larger and more powerful 1.8- and 2.0-litre units, the new Transporter really came fully into its own as an emergency vehicle, especially where ambulance conversions were concerned. The greater pulling power meant that there was little or no loss of performance when carrying the necessary extra equipment.

The Volkswagen factory built a range of emergency vehicles, including an extremely well equipped fast-response fire tender for use on

Above: Former Italian fire department Transporter with full-length roof-rack. Note typical Italian-specification white front indicators and the chromed door mirrors.

their own factory site at Wolfsburg. This vehicle was unusual in that it had roller-shutter sides, behind which was stowed a wide range of equipment to cope with just about any incident. Most fire service vehicles, however, were far more conventional in their design, continuing the trend set by the earlier Split-screen models. All styles of Type 2 continued to serve as a base on which to build a fire truck: both single-cab and crew-cab pick-ups were converted to ladder trucks, while panel vans, Kombis and even Deluxe Microbuses saw regular service.

But Bay-windows didn't only help to fight fires, for no sooner had the new model been launched than the factory included its own ambulance conversion in contemporary promotional material. However, that did not stop independent companies producing their own versions of the VW ambulance, some of which were based on high-roof models to allow more headroom for staff and patients alike. Even

today, over 20 years after the end of production, Bay-window ambulances are still in regular use (as are, of course, some Split-screen models!).

Naturally, it didn't take long for the Police forces of Europe to appreciate the finer points of the new Transporter range, the Kombi soon being pressed into regular service with the forces of law and order. Westfalia produced a number of Police-specification models built to the stringent DIN standards required by the German authorities.

Perhaps a little surprisingly, Bay-window emergency vehicles are less common today than the earlier Split-screen models. There's one probable reason for this, and another that's open to debate. Firstly, the original vehicles were so reliable and inexpensive to run that many authorities saw little reason to change their trusty old Split-screen models for the later design – hence the number of today's low-mileage survivors. Secondly, it's possible that the later Bay-window buses simply weren't built as well as their predecessors, so fewer have survived the test of time.

This 1978 fire vehicle was built by Volkswagen as a fast-response unit for attending emergencies ahead of the main fire brigade. Signwriting on door shows it to have been used within the factory.

This vehicle is extremely unusual in that it has roller-shutter doors on each side. It is based on a pick-up (note the locker and cooling vents on the rear quarters), with locker doors on both sides.

Second-generation fire vehicles are uncommon, making this 12-metre ladder truck — shown here during a training exercise — a rare sight. Note the spotlight mounted on the right front corner.

Opening the roller-shutters reveals a wide range of equipment to deal with every emergency. The rear section contains cutting and grinding gear, while the front houses oxy-acetylene equipment and a generator.

Generator unit slides out from load area on rails. Conversion was carried out by Volkswagen's own service workshops at Wolfsburg.

In the mid-'70s, the German Red Cross used these specially-insulated (note the small side door) Transporters to carry vital blood supplies.

Unusually for an emergency vehicle, this second-generation bus is a Deluxe model, complete with extra trim on the waistline and bumpers. Striped paint design of Frankfurt fire department is very distinctive.

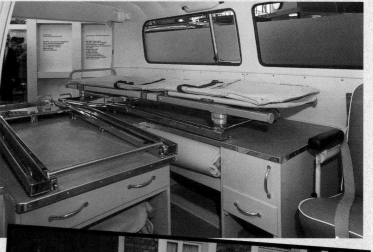

The interior space offered by the 'Bay-window' models suited an ambulance conversion. This example is a private conversion by an unknown company, on show at a trade exhibition in Germany.

Crew-cab, with small sliding window and full tilt and bows, was in use by the fire department at Frankfurt's Rhein-Main airport in the '70s. Note the dual exhaust pipes, suggesting that an Eberspächer petrol heater was installed, for keeping the vehicle warm while the engine was switched off.

The front bumper of most '70s ambulances had cut-outs to accommodate a pair of driving lights. This Red Cross vehicle has a normal bumper instead. Note the traditional ambulance side step beneath the sliding door.

Three second-generation ambulances in use by the Johanniter Unfall Hilfe, which, as lettering on the doors indicates, was part of a government organisation called Katastrophenschutz – meaning civil defence or disaster protection.

Volkswagen ambulances were widely used by the German military; this one carries full camouflage paintwork and the traditional large red crosses.

Baby paramedic vehicles were often equipped with incubator units to allow transportation of newly-born premature or sick babies from one hospital to another. Here just such a unit is being loaded into a mid-'70s example.

Deluxe bus (Type 24), with full trim and chromed bumpers, in use as a paramedic vehicle for attending incidents involving children or babies.

Photographed in late 1967, this prototype Westfalia police vehicle is shown equipped with a roof rack of the sort normally fitted to first-generation models — the folding ladder would normally be at the front of the rack when used with a sliding door.

A 1973 police conversion showing the correct style of Westfalia roof rack. Two-tone paintwork is relatively unusual for a police vehicle of this type.

A Transporter to strike terror into the heart of most drivers: it's a police radar unit built to catch speeding motorists! Divided front, with opening door to reveal the radar unit, was unique to this type of vehicle.

THREE'S COMPANY
The third generation makes its entrance

The Bay-window Transporters had been good workhorses and were far superior in virtually every respect to the first-generation models. However, there came a time when even the worthy Bays reached the end of the road, and that day came in May 1979 when Volkswagen released the first of a whole new line of transporters – the third-generation or T3.

The T3 models (also known as Type 25s) were radically different. There was hardly a curve to be seen anywhere on the bodywork and then, beneath the skin, torsion bar suspension made way for altogether more modern coil springs with wishbones (front) and semi-trailing arms (rear). Indeed, there was virtually nothing which could be interchanged with the earlier vehicles.

The new Transporter was, despite its box-like styling, considerably more aerodynamic than either the Bay-window or Split-screen buses. Whereas the earlier vehicles had been styled by eye, the new model was tested in a wind tunnel. Appearances can certainly be deceptive, for the T3 was more aerodynamically efficient than many passenger cars of the day!

Above: Introduced for the 1979 model year, the third-generation Transporter was a thoroughly modern design which built on the success of the previous models, but its angular styling was a radical departure.

The new Transporter was still not that frugal, being heavier than its predecessor yet still powered by essentially the same engine. It was wider (by some 5ins) and 2.5ins longer, although the height remained the same as the Bay-window models. The windscreen was some 21% larger, as was the sliding side door. The tailgate was enlarged, too, this being possible by reducing the height of the engine bay by over 6ins, meaning that it was now far easier to load goods into the rear. This reduction in engine bay height was possible because the old 'upright fan' engines of the Bays and Splits were no longer used; the new hydraulic-tappet 1.6-litre motor featured a cooling system not unlike that of the larger 2-litre units.

The new suspension system was a revelation, even if purists did take a while to accept the loss of the traditional torsion bars. Coil springs front and rear gave a far better ride, and allowed better use to be made of interior space. Rack and pinion steering was another vast improvement, the steering box of the original Transporters always having felt rather vague.

In 1980, Volkswagen did the unthinkable when it launched the 50bhp water-cooled in-line diesel-engined Transporter, this being joined in 1982 by a 1.9-litre water-cooled petrol engine. Later, in July 1985, the engine was enlarged to 2.1 litres and enjoyed the benefits of fuel injection. Coupled to new five-speed transmissions (with the all-wheel-drive Syncro joining the ranks in August the same year), these later water-cooled engines gave the Transporter very sprightly performance.

Still built to the traditionally high VW standards at Hannover, the third-generation Transporters were a hit from the word go. Their more conventional styling broadened their appeal in the marketplace and even the most die-hard Transporter owner of the 'old school' had to agree that these were indeed very fine vehicles. They may not have had the happy smiling face of the Split-screen buses or the friendly curves of the Bays, but their hearts were still in the right place (at the back, driving the rear wheels!).

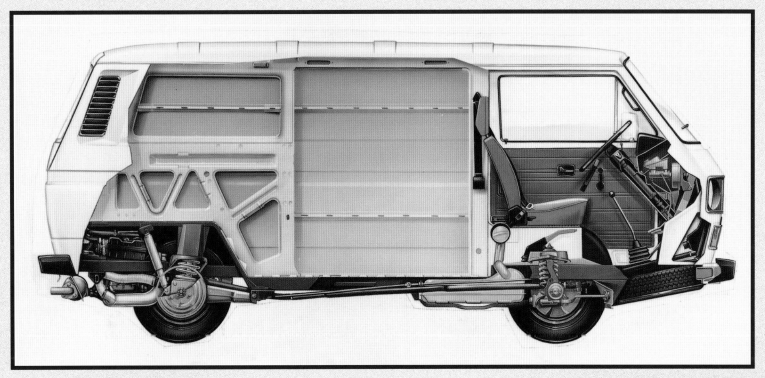

The new model followed the same basic concept, with a rear-mounted air-cooled engine and low loading platform, but did away with Porsche's well-proven torsion-bar suspension in favour of conventional coil springs.

The new design resulted in a useful increase in interior space, a factor which allowed the new Transporter to compete on an equal footing with contemporary rivals. One major advantage was the lower platform above the engine, making it easier to load goods from the rear.

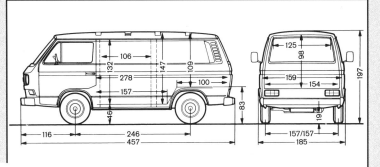

Volkswagen did the previously unthinkable by introducing water-cooled versions of the Transporter, in diesel form in 1980 and petrol form in 1982. A water-cooled model is easily distinguishable by its extra grille on the front panel.

The original Transporters came in for a lot of criticism from safety experts, especially in the USA. By the time the new model was introduced, safety legislation had moved on apace, necessitating the inclusion of deformable body sections and extra strengthening to protect the passengers in the event of a frontal impact.

Even in the late '70s, much of the assembly process was carried out by hand – a far cry from the popular image of a modern, robotised factory.

Completed bodyshells are seen here entering the first part of the paint process, to receive their anti-corrosion coating prior to spraying.

Assembly took place at the Hannover plant. The artistic photograph above shows a number of right-side body pressings on their way to the main assembly lines.

Modern (for the time) spraying equipment allowed paint colours to be changed at will – gone were the days of painting vehicles in batches of the same colour. Much of the final paint process, however, was still carried out by hand.

This photograph, taken in March 1989, shows a vehicle about to receive its engine and transmission assembly. Note the catalytic converter fitted to the exhaust system.

From the beginning of production, various body styles were available, including this Microbus, with full seating and two-tone paintwork.

With the rising popularity of double-cab pick-ups in the commercial market, Volkswagen introduced the latest version of this useful vehicle. Note the small storage locker behind the rear door. This particular example is powered by a diesel engine, based on that used in Volkswagen's passenger car range.

VW continued to enlarge the range by introducing various trim packages. This is the 'Carat', a high-specification Microbus with extra body trim, alloy wheels and plush interior trim.

Rare photograph of a pre-production 'Carat' — the model wasn't introduced until 1983 yet this photograph dates back to 1981. The front spoiler was matt black on production models, while the wheels normally carried VW-logo centre caps.

Powered by a 2.1-litre fuel-injected engine producing 112bhp, the top-of-the line vehicles were impressively fast, capable of around 100mph and accelerating from 0-60mph in under 12 seconds. The increased ride height tells us that the example above is a four-wheel-drive Syncro.

The Syncro was a fantastically versatile machine, which employed the latest all-wheel-drive technology. Drive was taken from the front of the transaxle forward to a second, front-mounted differential unit and from there to the front wheels. Differential locks gave the Syncro impressive off-road capabilities.

Even though this image (above) was printed at an angle to emphasise the slope, the Syncro was still capable of coping with terrain normally considered the territory of purpose-built off-road vehicles, such as Land-Rovers and Mercedes G-wagens.

Probably the ultimate Syncro was the Tristar, a high-specification model with body kit, plush interior trim and a wide range of options, including electric winch, bull-bars and alloy wheels.

As the end of production neared, Volkswagen released just 2500 of a special 'Limited' model, each numbered individually (a small badge on the door carries the serial number). This is number 81; the final example, number 2500, is on display in the VW Museum at Wolfsburg.

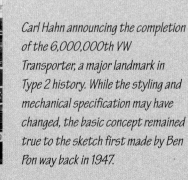

Carl Hahn announcing the completion of the 6,000,000th VW Transporter, a major landmark in Type 2 history. While the styling and mechanical specification may have changed, the basic concept remained true to the sketch first made by Ben Pon way back in 1947.

SOMETHING SPECIAL
Some unusual Type 25s

The new Transporters continued the tradition of versatility that was the hallmark of the VW commercial range from the earliest days. When the third-generation models were launched in 1979, the factory engineers immediately began work on producing a wide variety of special vehicles based on the new design.

First to appear were the traditional single-cab pick-ups, followed soon after by the crew-cab models and high-roofs. Such a line-up would be enough to please most manufacturers but the Wolfsburg design department was not one to rest on its laurels. Over the next few years, many unusual vehicles were built and shown to the public, some of which remained nothing more than interesting prototypes, while others went into limited production.

Volkswagen, or its approved independent specialists, such as Westfalia, built a wide variety of third-generation special models, including a comprehensive range of utility vehicles. Of these, one of the most unusual was a tilt-bed ('Kipper') version of the ever-practical crew-cab pick-up – normally such conversions were only carried out on single-cab models. There

Above: Jessen in Hamburg offered this aluminium bed conversion for the crew-cab, the advantages of which were ease of use and reduced weight.

was even an aluminium-bodied wide-bed pick-up built by Jessen of Hamburg, which offered the advantage of reduced all-up weight, thus allowing an increased payload.

Electrical companies involved with street-light maintenance could buy a Ruthmann-converted 'cherry picker' – this was a hydraulically-operated platform, which could be raised to allow a worker to service the lighting fixture, mounted on the rear platform of a single-cab pick-up.

Volkswagen mobile shop conversions had been popular since the '50s and the tradition continued into the '80s thanks to companies like Borco-Höhns, which produced a range of vehicles to suit this specialist (and lucrative) market. Refrigerated vans could also be supplied for use by butchers, fishmongers or florists who needed to keep their stock cool at all times.

Animals appear to have played an important part in the third-generation Transporter's life, if

some of the examples seen in this chapter are anything to go by! First of all, there was a special prototype tour bus built at Wolfsburg which was clearly aimed at companies running holiday packages in the big game reserves of Africa. It featured a raised viewing platform inside the bus and a 'pop-top' roof to allow passengers to get a clear (and safe!) view of the surrounding wildlife.

However, if the preservation of animals was not such a concern, you could have also bought a mobile kennel to transport your hunting dogs in style. Based on a crew-cab pick-up, this Swiss-built conversion probably remained a one-off prototype to show the potential. A far more professional conversion – and a stylish one, it must be said – was VW's own 'Jagdwagen', or hunting vehicle. This pick-up was built in the hope that it would appeal to wealthy hunters, most likely those from the Middle East.

No matter how unusual any of these conversions might have been, few can match the 'Schwimmfähiger Bus' of 1983. With its crankshaft-driven propeller and sealed water-proof body, this unique vehicle was a Transporter built to swim rivers and lakes.

Ladder truck was built by Volkswagen using a regular single-cab pick-up as a base. Unusually for such a conversion, it retains its drop-sides. Ladder is a 10-metre aluminium unit.

'Cherry Picker' by Ruthmann showing hydraulically-operated steadying legs. Such vehicles are popular with telephone and lighting contractors.

While single-cab tipper trucks are not too unusual, a crew-cab version is extremely rare. The controls for the hydraulic ram operating the bed are located in the side storage locker.

How do you carry long tree trunks on a pick-up? Just install a trailer axle unit! Carrying a load like this requires the removal of the tailgate.

Borco-Höhns produced this mobile shop based on a third-generation Transporter. Just like the Westfalia conversion of old, the side flaps open up to form a sales area.

This Swiss-based crew-cab features an unusual conversion: it's a mobile kennel! Aimed at the hunting fraternity, the vehicle serves to reinforce the versatility of the VW range.

An air-cooled engine can never freeze and, by placing it in the rear of the vehicle, over the driven wheels, you have the perfect basis for building a snow-plough. Such a vehicle is ideal for use in small rural communities.

Arrive at school in style aboard this school bus by Volkswagen. Based on a 1989 Kombi, its bright colour scheme and roof-mounted amber warning lights make it conspicuous for safety reasons.

The crew-cab 'Jagdwagen' (hunting vehicle) was built in limited numbers by the factory in its Kundendienst-Werkstatt, or special service workshops. Conversion incorporates a gun storage tray which slides underneath the pick-up bed.

This prototype, built by Volkswagen, shows how a Syncro Kombi might be used for African safari tours – the pop-up roof resembles that of a regular camper conversion, minus the sides. Bull-bar and electric winch cover all eventualities.

Just when you think you've seen it all – 1983 'Schwimmfähiger Bus' featured a propeller driven off the crankshaft, under the rear of the vehicle. All that remains to be asked is – 'Why?'

FIRE! POLICE! AMBULANCE!
Third-generation emergency vehicles

As with the first two generations of Transporter, the new model was soon adapted for use as an emergency vehicle of one type or another. Fire brigades, ambulance services and Police departments – all came to use the new Transporter almost from the start.

The radically improved design of the vehicle, compared to that of its forebears, meant that it was ideally suited to use on rough terrain – this being especially true when the all-wheel-drive Syncro model was introduced in August 1985. This superb vehicle was exactly what the emergency services in rural areas had been looking for as its advanced four-wheel-drive system gave the Transporter impressive off-road capabilities.

The new Transporter came to be used in various forms for fire-fighting duties. Some conversions were very similar to those carried out on early Split-screen fire trucks more than 20 years earlier in that they were little more than regular vans equipped with the most basic of equipment. Other conversions, however, were considerably more sophisticated, with specially-constructed bodywork to cater for a complex

Above: Volkswagen kept fully-equipped fire vehicles on the factory grounds in case of emergency. This photograph shows just such a vehicle, complete with all its fire hoses. Water pump unit is stored inside, behind the sliding door.

range of fire-fighting equipment. It almost goes without saying that the latest design of pick-up was also used to build ladder trucks for fire brigade applications.

It was probably in the role of an ambulance that the third-generation Transporter really shone, for its much-improved coil-sprung suspension gave a far superior ride to that of the older torsion bar set-up. The squarer body styling also allowed far better use to be made of the interior space, meaning that more equipment could be carried than was the case with the previous models. Although the external roof height was little or no different, inside there was slightly more headroom, making for a less cramped working environment, even without an optional high-roof conversion.

Volkswagen built its own ambulance conversion, which was put to good use by many authorities throughout the world. In addition,

several independent companies offered ambulances based around the T3 range, including Binz, whose name is often better associated with the first crew-cab conversions carried out on Split-screen pick-ups back in the '50s.

The new Transporter was also adopted by the Police, who doubtless also appreciated its redesigned suspension and improved interior space. The Police used the Transporter in various roles, from riot-control bus (our photograph shows one such vehicle equipped with a Dehler high-roof conversion) to personnel carrier. Indeed, it was a common sight (and still is in some regions) to see a roadside 'court' consisting of a Transporter in the familiar green and white German Police livery, complete with uniformed Police officials serving out instant 'justice' to speeding motorists.

Somehow, being apprehended by a fellow Volkswagen driver takes a little of the sting out of being caught for breaking the speed limit in Germany. On second thoughts, considering the size of speeding fines in that country, perhaps it doesn't. After all, not everybody who drives a Transporter for a living is a VW enthusiast!

This vehicle is painted in the colours of the US Army fire department at Hanau in Germany. It's seen here attending a traffic accident, presumably involving US army personnel.

Wolfsburg's fire brigade springs into action to demonstrate its latest acquisition, a 1984 Kombi. In the background is a VW LT-based fire truck.

An unusual conversion based on a Syncro crew-cab, which has been fitted with a Minimax fire extinguisher system. It's in service with the Hamburg fire department.

Italian volunteer fire brigade 4wd Kombi equipped with rare Syncro-only 16in wheels and wheel arch extensions. Note roof-mounted storage boxes and aluminium ladder.

The third-generation Transporter lent itself well to use as an ambulance, due to its greater interior space and more powerful engine options. This high-roof ambulance is unusual in that it has a special extended side door.

Interior of a high-roof ambulance conversion by Binz. Layout was little changed from that of the very earliest VW ambulances built some 35 years earlier.

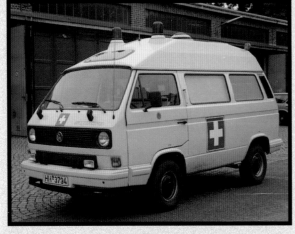

A rare Dehler high-top conversion for the Hamburg Police riot squad. Vehicle is a Syncro all-wheel-drive model.

Although several independent companies offered ambulance conversions, Volkswagen's own workshops produced a number of examples, such as this. Note the rear-facing bulkhead seats.

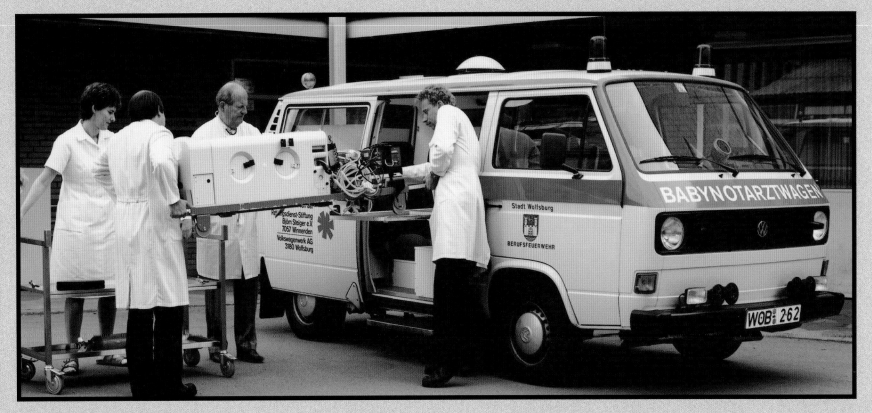

Third-generation baby paramedic unit continued the tradition laid down over the years of using Transporter-based ambulances for this vital task. Photograph shows incubator unit being unloaded.

Wiesbaden riot Police use these all-green Kombis — note the sliding side window and traditional roof-mounted blue light.

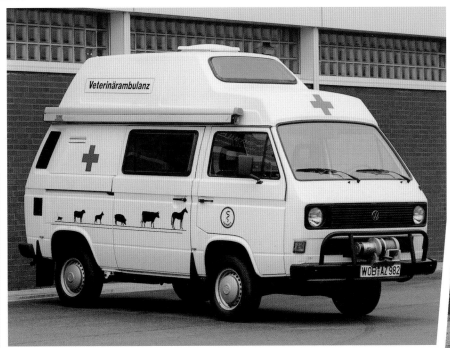

Even the animals get taken care of in style! This Syncro, complete with electric winch, was built by VW to show how such a vehicle might be put to use by a veterinary surgeon.

The usual Police colour scheme is green and white. Unit on roof combines emergency light with siren and loudspeaker.

CONTINUING THE TRADITION

Looking at the LTs, T4s and beyond

Back in the '50s, had anyone suggested that, one day, Volkswagen would build a commercial vehicle with the engine mounted at the front and driving the rear wheels, they would probably have been laughed out of the room. After all, Volkswagen's success had been founded on a well-proven layout of a rear-mounted, air-cooled engine driving the rear wheels. Any other design would have seemed like heresy back in Nordhoff's days. And as for a front-engined Transporter with front-wheel drive, well, who ever heard of such a crazy idea?

But times were changing and in the '70s Volkswagen was coming under attack from all sides. The Transporter could compete with most other manufacturers in the light delivery van market, but Volkswagen had nothing to offer in the light truck field. It was only a matter of time before VW announced an entirely new range of vehicles: the LT, short for Load Transport.

Launched in April 1975, the new range comprised just three basic vehicles: the LT28, LT31 and LT35. The figures indicate the laden weight of each truck – 2.8 tons, 3.1 tons and 3.5 tons. Only three versions of each were initially

Above: Four-wheel-drive version of the LT40 saw service with fire units in mountainous regions. Rosenbauer was the company responsible for this conversion, seen here tackling snow-covered slopes close to Salzburg, Austria.

offered by the factory, these being a delivery van, a drop-side pick-up and a bare chassis for use by independent body builders. For the first time, VW no longer built a Kombi version of their latest vehicle – that would be left to outside suppliers for the time being. There were just two engine options at this time: a 2-litre 75bhp petrol and a 2.7-litre 65bhp diesel developed for VW by Perkins in England.

Right from the start, the LT proved to be a hit and, over the years, the range grew to include more engine options and a choice of wheelbase. It was every bit as versatile as its smaller Transporter cousin and, between them, the two VW commercials proved to be very profitable.

However, VW was increasingly aware that the rear-engined Transporter was starting to show its age and in 1990 announced a whole new range: the T4s. These thoroughly modern vehicles bore no resemblance to their

predecessors other than having a Volkswagen badge on the nose. Front-engined, water-cooled, front-wheel-drive – the T4s were a whole new breed yet they still retained that VW versatility. With engine options all the way from small four-cylinder diesels up to VW's acclaimed 2.8-litre petrol VR6, the Eurovan, as it's known in the USA, proved to be another great success.

Like previous Transporters, T4s have been used in virtually every application and have appeared in every conceivable body style, including tipper trucks, crew-cabs and ambulances. Although considerably more sophisticated than any of its rear-engined cousins, the T4 has succeeded in keeping the Transporter legend alive and well.

But that isn't the end of the story for, in Europe, there has been another VW 'Transporter' of an altogether different kind: the Sharan. This sleek-looking MPV (Multi-Purpose Vehicle) is available with a wide range of engines and in top-of-the-line Carat trim is one of the most luxurious vehicles in its field. And just to prove that it's capable of maintaining the VW tradition, there have also been ambulance versions.

In April 1975 Volkswagen launched a new breed of commercial vehicle: the LT. Powered by a front-mounted water-cooled engine driving the rear wheels, the LT (two examples of which can be seen in the foreground) was a total departure from the VW norm.

LTs were assembled at Hannover, on production lines alongside those of the rear-engined Transporters. Here, the coil-sprung front suspension assemblies, complete with subframes, are being installed into LT pick-ups.

There is a touch of irony in this photograph for it shows the rear of a water-cooled LT fire truck, complete with an air-cooled VW-powered water pump. Times may have changed, but some things remain the same!

The LT proved to be every bit as popular as the rest of VW's commercial vehicle range, finding favour with the German fire brigade and seeing regular use alongside its rear-engined brethren.

The rugged nature of the LT made it ideal for use by organisations such as the Red Cross, which need vehicles they can rely on under all conditions.

German Bundeswehr (federal army) LT40 crew-cab makes an impressive machine, with its four-wheel drive and purposeful stance. They build them tough at Hannover!

It may not have the charm and character of a Split-screen Transporter, but the LT proved itself time and again as a dependable machine which could give years of service with emergency services across the world.

Military ambulance conversion has many interesting features, including the remote air filter mounted alongside the windscreen. It's a far cry from the first VW ambulance built some 38 years earlier!

A VW-built LT with a Drandt refrigerated body conversion helps to prove that the LT had lost none of its forebears' versatility.

In 1990, Volkswagen launched a new Transporter range, known by many as the T4 (ie, fourth-generation Transporter). A thoroughly modern vehicle, it's a far cry in every respect from the Samba shown here for comparison.

The T4 couldn't be more different from its predecessors if it tried! Not only is the engine located in the front but it's mounted transversely, driving the front wheels through a transaxle unit. Several engine options are used, including VW's superb 2.8-litre VR6 and this 2.4-litre diesel.

The T4 also went into use with the emergency services. This is a minibus vehicle used by the Hannover fire department.

A T4 fire truck, complete with extinguisher system, continues the tradition laid down by the original fire trucks of the '50s. This conversion, by H&S, may lack character but it's undeniably purposeful.

Ambulance conversions were always going to be part of the T4's history if it was to continue in the great VW tradition. This Transporter is in use with the German Red Cross at Helmstedt.

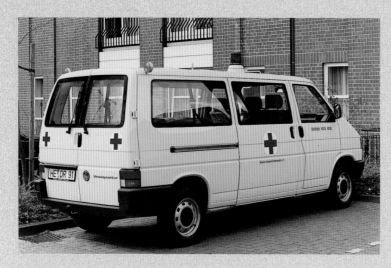

The German Police put the new Transporter into use as soon as it became available and examples can be seen all across the country in the well-known green-and-white livery.

The T4 can be ordered in a variety of body styles, including a panel van and, as shown here, a pick-up. Front-engine, front-wheel drive layout allows the height of the pick-up bed to be kept to a minimum for ease of use.

Double-cab pick-up with tipper conversion is primarily aimed at the construction industry.

'Our environment must remain clean!', says the slogan on the door. With a snow plough attachment and gritter body, this T4 is ready for the worst winter conditions.

The new-generation Transporter has even been converted into a mobile shop or, as in this case, a mobile bake-house, selling freshly-baked pretzels by the roadside.

Hookipa was a factory-built prototype conversion designed to appeal to the young at heart. Inside, its seating could be converted to form sleeping accommodation, while the special integral roof rack could house a pair of wind-surf boards. This unique vehicle can be seen in the VW Museum.

The Optare City-Pacer was a British-built conversion based on the chassis of an LT for use by local bus companies. Its dramatic styling sets it apart from its rivals.

The latest vehicle which can be considered a part of the Transporter family is the Sharan. A joint venture between VW, Ford and SEAT, the Sharan is available with several engine options, including the VR6 motor. Sharans have proved popular as paramedic vehicles, such as this.

CARRY ON CAMPING

The world's best-loved home from home

Has there ever been a more successful or better-loved camper than the Volkswagen? In the early '50s several independent companies, including Westfalia in Germany, felt the Transporter was the perfect basis for a low-cost, easy-to-drive motor caravan which would appeal to families the world over. At this time a new spirit of adventure made caravanning a popular pastime, but not everyone owned a car capable of towing a caravan and few had the space or funds to make ownership of a separate car and caravan a viable proposition.

The answer lay with VW's Transporter, a vehicle small enough to be driven to and from work every day yet large enough to be converted into a motorised caravan for all the family to enjoy. Virtually square and with not an inch of wasted space, it was the perfect shape for conversion. Large side doors made entry and exit easy, while the compact rear-mounted engine meant there was no wasted space in the cab – or a hump to clear a conventional transmission.

It didn't take long for companies like Westfalia to appreciate the Transporter's possibilities, especially in Kombi trim with side

Above: A nice example of a '66 Westy, with Westfalia elevating 'pop-top' roof and matching Westy roof rack. Sun visor over windscreen is an after-market accessory.

windows. Most other motor caravans of the time were built from delivery vans and were unsophisticated by comparison. It's easy to forget in these days of well-equipped commercial vehicles just how crude, slow, noisy and smelly post-war vans could be!

The challenge for any would-be camping conversion business was how to make best use of the internal space. Every company seemed to have its own concept of the perfect camper, but it wasn't until someone (history doesn't record who) first installed an elevating roof that the vehicle's true potential could be realised. No longer did adults have to stoop, bent-necked, inside the little VW! Elevating roofs also offered the opportunity to install child-sized bunk beds, turning the vehicle into a true four- or even five-berth camper. Westfalia were among many to market side awnings – tent-like structures which clipped to the side of the camper, doubling the amount of sleeping space.

When the second-generation Transporter was launched, the camper market expanded still further, for the new model offered more space inside and a higher standard of equipment. When Volkswagen finally installed a larger engine in 1971, the camping industry breathed another sigh of relief, for the poor old 1600cc Beetle-derived engine had been struggling to cope with the added weight of the average conversion. And remember, the first examples from the early '50s would have been powered (in the loosest sense of the term) by nothing more than a 25bhp engine of just 1131cc!

With each successive redesign of the Transporter, the possibilities for use as a well-equipped camper increased. More space, more power and more comfort on long journeys – the new breed of campers have it all. But somehow, none of the current models – not even those built by Westfalia in Germany or Winnebago in the USA – can ever match the original Split-screens or Bay-windows for character. They represented a whole new outlook on life, offering families the opportunity to take off for a weekend at a moment's notice.

There is no more famous a name in the world of Volkswagen campers than Westfalia, a German company located at Wiedenbrück. In 1994, a group of enthusiasts formed the Westfalia Registry, celebrating the occasion with a visit to the factory.

A Westfalia camper is loaded into the hold of VW's cargo ship bound for the USA in 1962. This was a laborious task, as each vehicle had to be individually loaded and lashed to the deck by hand.

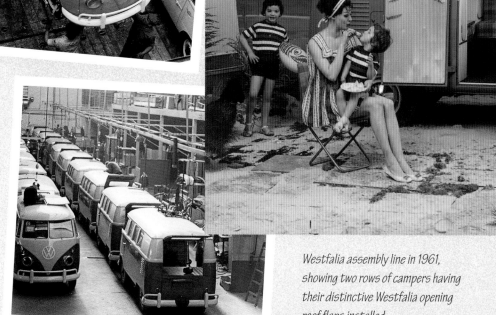

Westfalia assembly line in 1961, showing two rows of campers having their distinctive Westfalia opening roof flaps installed.

Dreadfully staged publicity photograph shows prototype 'Westy' in studio setting — sorry, in the south of France . . .

The little Puck caravans are the perfect complement for a Split-screen camper, offering extra space — and a matching pop-top roof!

The perfect camping scene, with sunshine, great scenery, a pair of 1966 Westies and an Eriba Puck caravan in tow for good measure.

In the studio once more, tiny Westfalia tent provided a small amount of extra space, something which the early Split-screen campers otherwise lacked.

Westfalia pop-top (left) meets Dormobile (right) with side-hinged elevating roof — two ways to solve a common problem: how to increase headroom in the early Type 2.

Because space was so limited inside, it was commonplace for manufacturers to mount certain items so that they could be accessed from outside the vehicle. In this case, the young lady is showing us the sink unit in this Westfalia. Note the double bed alongside the unit.

Many campers have become the pride and joy of their owners, with most, if not all, benefiting from the addition of accessories. Julian Hunt's '62 features Safari windows and cab roof rack.

Believed to be the oldest Devon motor caravan in existence, this 1956 camper was owned by Gerald Toone in England. Note that it doesn't feature a 'walk-through' front bulkhead.

Side-hinged Dormobile roof was a major advance over tiny Westfalia pop-top, allowing a whole family to sleep inside with a reasonable degree of comfort.

Typical Devon interior, with swing-out cooker and cupboard unit. 'Walk-through' bulkhead makes life a lot easier, allowing driver and passenger to get to the rear without having to step outside into the rain.

This 1978 second-generation Westfalia camper is rare in that it has the small pop-top roof more normally associated with earlier models. Westy roof rack completes the 'vintage' look.

Westfalia interiors are very distinctive, with their high-quality laminate finish and excellent attention to detail. This is a combined fridge and sink unit. In the background is the cooker.

This Westfalia Helsinki conversion dates back to 1973. Note the front-hinged elevating roof — later models were hinged at the rear, the static section of the roof being over the cab.

Another Westfalia tradition was the use of louvred opening side windows, as seen here. There are a number of interesting features on this '78 camper, including a front-mounted spare-wheel box and bumper extension and an automatic side step, which pops out as the door is opened.

Devon was one of the most prolific of all British camper manufacturers. This Devon Eurovette was bought new by Bob Sexton back in 1973 and hired out as part of his business. Despite its working life, it remained in perfect condition until it was eventually sold some 20 years later.

The Moonraker was one of Devon's most popular conversions, but still retained the trademark striped elevating roof and swing-out cooker unit.

Moonraker interior showing the elevating roof in position. Typically, Devon fittings of this era featured genuine wood trim with grey laminate doors and work surfaces.

Devon Sundowner was a high-spec Kombi-based conversion, with low-profile elevating roof and Westy-style louvred side windows. Check those flared trousers!

Devonette was Devon's bargain-basement model, based on a Kombi or panel van. Elevating roof was an option which most customers specified, preferring the added expense to the alternative of a stiff neck . . .

Many camper conversions offered the opportunity to hang a child's hammock across the cab, above the front seats, an option which obviously proved popular with these two young campers!

Dutch Kemperink long-wheelbase box van conversions have often been snapped up for use as campers. Double side doors and large windows mean that the interior is light and airy, while roof box offers even more storage space.

Sun, sea, sand and a Westy! What more can anyone ask?

A 1968 Westfalia 'on vacation' in Iceland.

Prize for the most unlikely name goes to Westfalia's 'Joker' — a high-top conversion based on the third-generation Transporter. Jokers are among the most popular of all late-model campers.

The Sunseeker was one of several British conversions and featured plenty of storage space, along with a side-hinged elevating roof. Some companies offered DIY kits for home installation.

The Devon tradition continued into a third generation with the Eurovette (left) and Caravette (right). The former featured a high-top conversion, the latter a pop-top.

VW campers come in all shapes and sizes. This is a Karmann conversion based on a 1982 Transporter and has more the look of an American motorhome than a traditional VW camper. While it may not win any beauty prizes, it's certainly not short on space.

The Weekender was a conversion by D'Ieteren in Brussels, the official Belgian VW importer and distributor. Note the step cut into the side, above the rear wheel, allowing easier access to the roof storage area and side awning.

A crew-cab is relatively rare, but a crew-cab motorhome is even more unusual! This is the Road Ranger by Dr Höhn GmbH of Ingelfingen in Germany.

'I see no ships!'. Karosseriewerke Weinsberg built this camper, known as the Terra. The company also offered Fiat-based conversions for the German market.

Tischer pick-up conversion features a removable camper body. 'Demountable' conversions such as this are popular in the USA, where they are more normally based on large American pick-ups rather than a humble Volkswagen.

Clearly this young lady loves her Dehler Profi high-top camper. Its futuristic styling made it a popular conversion. Note the insulated 'bubble' side windows and body kit.

Yet another Devon conversion (above). High-top conversions are popular on late-model campers, offering greater headroom with none of the weather-proofing problems often associated with elevating-roof campers.

There is more than one way to build a camper, as this line-up of British conversions shows. From the left: Devon, Richard Holdsworth, Auto-Sleeper and Autohomes (UK) Ltd.

Liberty Van by Boehm in Germany echoed the styling of many custom vans in the USA, with its large side window, stepped roofline and flashy paint. Alloy wheels add the finishing touch to this extrovert conversion.

The Lyding camper was also based on a crew-cab and offered plenty of interior space.

Short on style, large on space. Even the LT got a look in, thanks to Devon. Somehow it doesn't have quite the charm of a Split-screen Westy. . .

With the advent of the T4 range, the camper market received a shot in the arm. In America, the famous Winnebago company produced this superbly equipped motorhome based on a T4 Transporter, which was sold through VW agencies across the USA.

CUSTOM CREATIONS

Some people are never satisfied!

When you consider just how many Transporters are on the road, it's quite easy to understand why some people might wish to make theirs stand out from the crowd. For most, adding a few accessories or changing the colour scheme would be sufficient, but for others such simple measures aren't enough.

Customising – the art of personalising a car or van so that it reflects the owner's tastes – has always existed in one form or another. As far back as the early '50s, companies would repaint their Transporters to make sure they couldn't be missed as they drove down the street, while accessory companies in Germany produced a wide range of 'bolt-ons' to help owners personalise their vehicles. But it was in America in the '60s that the idea of customising Volkswagen vans really took off.

Among the first customs were the wildly-painted 'hippy' buses of the love and peace Woodstock generation. Frequently covered in psychedelic imagery, these crazy hand-painted vans and campers typified the carefree ideology of their owners. Few of the original Flower Power buses survive today, for most of them were

Above: Jerry Jess's hippy bus, called 'Bessie', was created in the '60s and followed the rock band Grateful Dead all over America. This genuine 'Dead Head' bus is one of the rare survivors of a crazy era.

pretty beaten up at the time and have long since been sent on their way to the great rock festival in the sky. However, there are a few to be seen, among them 'Bessie', a hand-painted bus originally owned by a 'Dead Head' – a fan of American rock group Grateful Dead. Bessie now belongs to arch bus fanatic Jerry Jess and is destined to be restored to its former glory.

But simply splashing on some crudely executed flower or rainbow designs is not what true customising is all about – at least, not as far as some enthusiasts are concerned. For them, it's necessary to take things a stage or two further, with extensive body reworking a top priority. One of the first tricks, and certainly one of the most time-consuming, was to shorten a Transporter by the simple expedient of slicing a few feet out of the middle – usually the section occupied by the side doors. Welding the two remaining halves back together would result in a

rather comic short-wheelbase vehicle with somewhat strange handling characteristics. Of course, some people took things a stage further again and used the section they cut out to lengthen a second bus!

Once that idea caught on, there was no stopping people. Chopping the roof pillars to lower the roof line, or even slicing the roof off altogether, became popular pastimes. Whether creating roofless pick-ups from vans, or stretched limousine-like buses from ageing Microbuses, there appears to be no end to people's imagination and ingenuity. Many such conversions have been, admittedly, rather crude in execution but all served as a reflection of the owner's desire to be different.

Today, the trend is towards lowering the suspension, fitting a more powerful engine and finishing the body with flawless paintwork. Inside, there's an emphasis on keeping things simple, with little or no creature comforts other than a hugely powerful stereo system! Conservative as this may sound compared with the cut'n'shut vehicles of days gone by, some of today's custom buses are among the wildest ever built.

The first 'custom' Transporters were almost certainly the psychedelic hippy buses of the Woodstock era. With drug-induced designs, they were the symbol of rebellion.

What looks to be a mid-'50s European model (the bus still has semaphores, which have been covered over with after-market turn signals) has been given the full hippy treatment – applied by hand, naturally.

Not only early buses received the hippy attention – the later Bay-windows respond just as well to a touch of the paint brush.

Of course, you can always two-tone your bus, keeping the top half stock while going crazy on the lower half...

Alternatively, don't even bother to paint your bus — or do anything at all, preferably for years and years. A regular sight at Southern California VW shows, this bus thumbs its nose at convention.

Can't be bothered to paint your bus yourself? Well, why not ask everyone else to help you out?

However for some, the idea of driving a mobile wreck has no appeal. This 23-window Samba looks good enough to eat, rolling on its set of Porsche wheels.

Resto-Cal treatment looks great on a bus — dropped suspension, BRM-style wheels and flawless two-tone paintwork result in a pleasing blend of custom and resto.

Bruno Courbon has every right to look happy — who wouldn't be while driving a show-winning Samba and viewing the road through a pair of Safari windows?

In total contrast to the hippy buses, many Type 2s have been built with show winning in mind. These buses are perfect examples of detailing gone mad!

For many purists, the sound of an air-cooled flat-four is sweet music enough. For others, it takes a battery of amplifiers and speakers to achieve aural satisfaction!

Full Deluxe body trim sets off the two-tone metallic blue paint a treat on this Kombi. Cloudless Las Vegas skies make the paintwork glow.

Is a Split-screen too slow or unsophisticated for your tastes? How about this custom T4, complete with body kit, alloy wheels and wall-to-wall surfboards?

And talking of Type 2s being slow, you could always drop a Chevrolet V8 into the back of your Vanagon (US third-generation Transporter) for some real horsepower!

A more conventional transplant would be to install a modified, dual-carburettor VW engine in an early bus. This example needs all the help it can get because it's now been stretched and turned into the Limobus! Bob Koch of California built the Limobus as a rolling advert for his business. It now resides in Belgium.

Of course, you could always go the other way and take a few feet out of the middle of your Samba. This wild custom has been cut'n'shut, lowered and detailed to the max for the ultimate in show-stopping looks.

Pick-ups can get the chop, too. In fact, shortening a pick-up is a whole lot less work than chopping a van, but the effect is just as striking.

The side windows give the game away as to how this bus was shortened: the entire side-door section has been removed. Wheelie bar on the back helps keep the nose down under acceleration!

The long and the short of it! In 1966, a body repair shop in California decided to build a long-wheelbase Type 2 using the front half of a rare double-door Transporter and the rear of an equally rare 23-window Samba. So what did they do with the 'left-overs'? Why, they welded them together to make an ultra-short van, of course!

What a great way to advertise a product! Shorter-than-short pick-up looks small enough to gather up under your arm.

Randy Ingersoll had to go a stage or two further — he owns a stretched six-wheel pick-up on which he carries his shortened Bay-window Transporter! Only in California . . .

For many, a crew-cab is the ultimate starting point for building a custom. Full-length side step is an unusual accessory on a pick-up, being more normally seen on buses.

Of course, with crew-cabs being rare, you could always build one out of a Transporter, like this. Note how the original side door is still in use, to gain access to a storage area behind the cab.

Even your kids don't need to be left out of the fun! This pair of down-sized buses was spotted at a California VW show.

The alternative custom pick-up! A cut-down 'barn-door' Transporter which has then been slammed, fitted with home-made fender skirts and hand-painted.

By way of total contrast is another cut-down Transporter, this time one which looks ready to see some drag-strip action. Roll-cage is a sensible addition while full-length tonneau cover is practical.

Despite being designed as a utilitarian workhorse, the VW pick-up lends itself well to the full custom treatment. Chromed bumpers, window frames and Safaris look great against peach paint.

Yet another cut-down van, this time with a unique paint job!

One for the nostalgia fans: Darrell Vittone, famous VW drag racer of the early '70s, used this crew-cab to tow his race car. Check out the EMPI Sprintstar wheels.

This amazing pick-up features full Deluxe trim and Safari windows. However, it is also equipped with hydraulic suspension!

TRANSPORTER PUBLICITY

Promoting the Volkswagen Transporter

Volkswagen has always prided itself in publishing some of the most attractive, informative and, as it has turned out, collectable of all promotional material. Even as far back as the early '50s, it printed extremely detailed and well-illustrated brochures depicting the Transporter range in a variety of guises.

The very first brochures came with black and white cover imagery but inside there were colour illustrations showing Transporters in their natural working environment, as sign-written delivery vans going about their daily duties. These early brochures are extremely rare and fetch very high prices. However, for many, the most attractive publicity material of all came in the mid-'50s when Volkswagen used the services of Bernd Reuters, a highly acclaimed artist whose technique has remained unique to this day. His stylised, colourful images of buses and vans decorated the covers of VW brochures for many years, while inside there were detailed cut-away illustrations showing how the vehicles were built and how they could be adapted.

While the Reuters brochures undoubtedly have the most visual appeal, there has been a

Above: The very first Transporter brochure, dated early 1950. It was a simple monochrome publication which showed some of the prototype vans in detail. Lieferwagen means 'delivery vehicle'.

huge variety of publicity material produced by VW over the years. Whenever a new model was launched, a matching brochure was printed, even if the vehicle was only to be produced in small numbers for a limited market. This way, it's possible to find brochures for ambulances and fire tenders, ladder trucks, refrigerated delivery vans – even Police vehicles. In fact, it's probably true to say that no other company has ever published such a wide range of material relating to its products.

Throughout the later '50s and the '60s, the style of brochures changed. No longer were people happy to see what a Transporter might have looked like had an artist designed it; they wanted to see what the vehicle really looked like, warts and all. Artwork gradually gave way to photography and, for some at least, the brochures began to lose their appeal.

When the Bay-window models were launched

in the summer of 1967, the style of the publicity material changed dramatically – gone were the rather fanciful designs of the past and in their place were often very plain brochures with single-colour covers and little in the way of illustration. However, the overall design did frequently vary from market to market, the European brochures tending on the whole to be rather ordinary, while those produced for the American market were usually brighter and more attention-grabbing.

It was only when the third-generation Transporters were released that brochure covers generally began to show vehicles in all their glory once more. This time, however, the photographs were frequently taken in studios rather than in a working environment.

In addition to the sales brochures, Volkswagen has also published many other items depicting the Transporter in one form or another, including road safety education leaflets, colouring books and games for children, all of which are prized by today's collectors. There was even a special magazine called 'Flotter Transport', which served to show how versatile the VW commercial vehicles were.

Inside the 1950 sales brochure there were several beautiful photographs showing early Transporters in their natural working environment.

By December 1950, the sales brochure had become altogether more stylish, with Reuters' famous artwork making its appearance for the first time.

Dating from late 1950 or early 1951,
this brochure depicted a Deluxe bus in the popular colour combination of
Chestnut Brown and Sealing Wax Red. Note the full Deluxe trim, as later used on Samba models.

In stark contrast to driving manuals offered by rival manufacturers, those given by VW to each new Transporter owner were works of art, with detailed cut-away drawings. These examples were issued in June and November 1950.

The first Samba
publicity
appeared in
September 1951,
the brochure
featuring more
of Reuters'
beautiful artwork
on the cover.

The February 1951
brochure showed
the VW family,
side by side.
Muted colours
were typical of
the era.

With the launch
of the pick-up
came a new
brochure — this
example was
published in
July 1952.

VW-PRITSCHENWAGEN
»PICK-UP«

Das VW-Taxi

Compared with other VW brochures of the time, that issued to promote the VW
taxi was austere in design and presentation. Date of publication was June 1953.

Die VW-Transporter

Die VW-Transporter

Mit ihm fährt der Erfolg

The brochures above, both depicting the Transporter range, form an interesting contrast in style. The first, dated early 1955, featured Reuters artwork; the second, from 1956, was by VW's new artist, Preis.

A rare brochure (above) from 1959 shows a different style again from previous hand-outs. The slogan can be roughly translated as 'Success drives with him'.

The Larger Volkswagen for Large Families and Small Parties

Volkswagen Station Wagon and De Luxe Station Wagon

Ein VW-Pritschenwagen zum Selbstbasteln

The cover above is actually from a cut-out paper kit given out by VW dealers to promote the pick-up: 'A pick-up for the hobbyist'.

'The larger Volkswagen for larger families and small parties', says the headline of this August 1958 American brochure. Artwork is once again by Preis.

The 1959 Ambulance had its own special brochure, with some very stylish cover artwork by Preis.

This beautiful artwork adorned the cover of the 1959/60 Microbus brochure.

The 1957/58 brochure shown above was, as the artwork suggests, primarily aimed at the agricultural market.

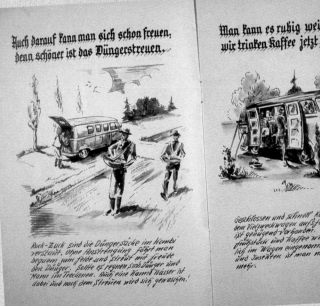

Farmer Alfred Gebhardt loved his Transporter so much that he produced his own little hand-drawn booklet, which he then sent to Volkswagen. VW was so impressed that it was reproduced and published as an amusing give-away in the late '50s.

It's official: Father Christmas drives a Volkswagen! In Germany, VW published a magazine entitled 'Flotter Transport' (roughly translated as 'Rapid Transport'), the Christmas 1960 edition of which showed Santa arriving in style. Inside there was a great game: you had to count how many Volkswagens you could find in the picture. Well, how many can you see?

Children weren't left out of the fun in 1961, for VW of America produced this little booklet which contained pictures to colour and games to play.

How many people can you get in a Microbus? Volkswagen's advertising of 1962 suggested nine, but, in the UK at least, eight (including the driver) was the legal limit.

An attractive brochure (right) for the Samba, dated January 1963.

Wie lange arbeitet eigentlich so ein VW-Transporter?

In 1964 Volkswagen carried out a campaign to find the oldest working Transporters in Germany. The winner was a 1950 model — and the prize? A new Transporter. Today, most enthusiasts would prefer to keep the original!

Rare hand-drawn mock-up of a February 1965 leaflet, shown with the finished item.

Promotional material was even produced for vehicles like the fire truck. This example was published in January 1963 and depicts two such vehicles outside a fire station.

The Volkswagen family of trucks.

A simple, yet attractive, brochure (left) handed out by American dealers in 1968 depicted the majority of the Transporter range. As with a clever design published in 1976 (below), American publicity material tended to emphasise the amount of space inside a VW bus.

The VW Wagon.

It's more than you bargained for.

First and last. The new Bay-window model, launched in August 1967, spawned a whole new style of brochure. The first of the new design is shown here with the last Split-screen brochure, printed in January 1967.

la proverbiale sicurezza VOLKSWAGEN anche come...

This is an example of Italian publicity material promoting the VW bus for use as a schoolbus. The date is September 1968.

As American manufacturers were having to think about downsizing their station wagons to cope with rising fuel prices, VW smugly suggested that everyone should take the bus — the Volkswagen bus!

A September 1978 brochure depicting a Police Kombi in action at the scene of a road accident.

To help promote road safety to children, a series of colouring books was published in the mid-'70s. It's no coincidence that all the vehicles shown are Volkswagens — after all, brand loyalty starts young!

IN A WORLD FULL OF SHRINKING WAGONS, IT'S MORE FUN TO TAKE THE BUS.

Der neue Volkswagen Transporter.

Der Wasserboxer-Motor im Volkswagen Transporter.

Volkswagen Kombi. Wenn es einmal gekracht hat.

Volkswagen TriStar syncro.

Die große Verkehrs Familie

Das Verkehrs-Arbeitsheft für den Schulanfänger

NAME

KLASSE

With the arrival of the third-generation Transporter came yet another series of brochures. They had little of the style of the classic publications of the '50s and '60s. In October 1982 VW printed the first brochure (left) to depict a water-cooled Transporter. As far as many enthusiasts were concerned, the end of the classic Transporter line was in sight.

Quite probably the most desirable of all the late-model family, the TriStar Syncro warranted its own brochure, this example being published in September 1987.

Here is the Devon CARAVETTE

MOTORISED CARAVAN ON THE VOLKSWAGEN MICRO-BUS

the ideal holiday home . . . complete and ready for YOU!

British motor caravan specialist, Devon, produced some wonderful period brochures; this one was published in 1959 or 1960. It was very factual, yet attractive in its simplicity.

E-Z Camper

★ AMERICA'S MOST POPULAR SPORT

Volkswagen Van with E-Z Camper ready to go.

Convenient ice box with 50 lb. capacity.

The '50s American E-Z (pronounced Eee-Zee) Camper conversion was similar in many respects to the Westfalia, with its plentiful storage space and combined fridge and sink units. Opening side windows featured fly screens, just like Westfalia's.

★ *Camping fun*

WITH CONVENIENT & LUXURIOUS FACILITIES ALL IN ONE COMPACT UNIT!

E-Z CAMPER WILL CONVERT YOUR VOLKSWAGEN 211 VAN TO A WONDERFUL WEEKEND CABIN ON WHEELS!

The DEVON MOTOR CARAVANS

DESIGNED AND PRODUCED BY DEVON CRAFTSMEN ON THE VOLKSWAGEN

By 1965 Devon had added colour to its brochures. The photographs show signs of having been retouched by hand – the red of the camper is far brighter than one would normally have expected!

This 1964 Canterbury Pitt conversion was said to be 'open plan' and offered no fewer than eight different seating/sleeping layouts. The cooker unit was mounted on the door but there was no sink, just a water tank and separate bowl.

With or without ELEVATING ROOF

CANTERBURY'S "OPEN PLAN"

1965 VOLKSWAGEN PITT *Moto-Caravan*

Patents Nos. 832678 829694

PMC Division

OCTOBER, 1964

CANTERBURY INDUSTRIAL PRODUCTS (AVELEY) LTD.

CANTERBURY HOUSE, ARISDALE AVENUE, SOUTH OCKENDON, ROMFORD, ESSEX Telephone - South Ockendon 3456 (10 lines) Cables - Cantacar

THE VOLKSWAGEN DORMOBILE 4-BERTH CARAVAN
PRICE £915 COMPLETE (U.K.) *(No Purchase Tax)* Dual Colours Extra

The Martin Walter Dormobile conversion was ingenious, being equipped with 'Dormatic' folding seats which offered a variety of internal layouts. Dormobiles were available through UK Volkswagen agents.

Later Dormobile brochure — this one dates from November 1976 — showed Martin Walter's conversion on a Bay-window Transporter. Forward location of elevating roof was a trademark of Dormobile, leaving space for a roof rack at the rear. Cooker was located behind passenger seat.

Volkswagen of Australia published this brochure showing the range of conversions — including a Dormobile – available through its dealerships.

We couldn't resist including this great photograph from a 1970 American VW camper brochure. Was Volkswagen of America trying to suggest that the Westfalia tent resembled a wig-wam?

As with other third-generation brochures, this 1982 American publication (below) lacked the style of earlier designs. It was very clinical in its presentation — a far cry from the charm of the Devon publicity material of 20 years before.

BE THRIFTY.

BUY A VW DIESEL VAN.

TODAY'S BEST CHOICE.

The end of the road for the last of the 'real' (ie, rear-engined) Transporters came in February 1992 when VW lauched the limited edition model, along with its stylish commemorative brochure.

Last Edition.

The Bay-window model may have reached the end of the road in Europe in 1979, but it continued to be built in South America – even in diesel-engined form, as the above 1982 brochure proves.

mortuário

O Furgão VW adaptado para carro mortuário é dividido em 2 andares, por plataformas metálicas especiais, um com acesso pelas portas laterais, e o outro pela porta traseira. Cada andar contém duas urnas mortuárias, que deslizam sôbre roletes giratórios de aço. Uma divisão metálica separa hermèticamente a cabina do compartimento de transporte. A pintura é em côr padrão polícia, com os dizeres "Polícia", na frente e atrás.

carro funerário

A Kombi funerária é equipada com uma mesa de aço montada sôbre trilhos, e que desliza para fora do carro. Uma divisão metálica, com visor, separa o compartimento do motorista.
As janelas do compartimento de carga são fixas.
A pintura interna é na côr cinza, e a externa pode ser branca ou preta.

Finally, if you think you cannot live without a VW bus, think again. The first brochure is for a Split-screen mortuary van, complete with special metal caskets, while the second is for a Kombi hearse. The perfect end for a Transporter enthusiast?

BUSES ABROAD
The Transporter at work, rest and play

Throughout its life, the Volkswagen Transporter has been put to an amazing variety of uses and has been photographed in all kinds of situations, some comic, some serious. In this chapter, we have gathered together a large number of images which help to celebrate the affection in which the Transporter has been held.

The collection ranges from period photographs depicting delivery vans at work in the '50s to those taken while the Type 2 was subjected to crash testing to prove how it could

A nicely restored 1952 Kombi (above) which still retains its original three-dimensional 'sign-writing'. A sign-written trailer made from the salvage of a damaged Transporter (below) makes a great publicity tool, especially when towed behind a matching panel van.

meet the most stringent of US safety regulations. We can see pick-ups rebuilt to resemble steam locomotives, a van used to create a roadside chapel, Deluxe Microbuses in use as airport transfer vehicles – even a bus in

the role of 'Oscar The Talking Police Car'!

And then there are the gimmicks designed for the bus collector who has everything: the Samba mailbox, Split-screen sunglasses, hand-painted tiles, clothing – the list of what is available to the Transporter enthusiast is almost endless. Clearly, if there's any money left over after restoring your prized Volkswagen, there are plenty of ways in which it can be spent.

But, while we are on the subject of money, the final word must go to a piece of modern 'art'. 'Das Rudel' ('The Pack' in English) is, officially, the world's most expensive Volkswagen. It forms part of a 'sculpture' by German artist Joseph Beuys. Back in the '70s, it was originally estimated to be worth around DM 1.5 million, a ludicrous figure by any standards. However, in 1993 this highly acclaimed piece sold for an amazing DM 16.5 million (that's approximately £6 million, or just under $10 million)!

And what does this sculpture consist of? Is it made of pure gold? Sadly no, for it's nothing more than a rusty VW bus 'towing' a chain of sleds – and people accuse we VW enthusiasts of being crazy!

The '4711 eau de cologne' factory bought the very first Transporter to be sold outside the factory way back on 8 March 1950. Ten years later to the very day, the same company took delivery of another new Transporter, the occasion being marked by a small celebration.

They may have been stationed in Germany but you couldn't keep US servicemen away from their motor sport. Photo from March 1966 shows a Kombi being used as the timing control at a drag race meeting held on Ramstein air base.

A well-known photo taken in the early '50s outside the gates of the then new VW factory in Brazil, showing a locally built Samba complete with roof vent above the windscreen.

A freshly sign-written 1959 pick-up advertising the latest drink to hit the pubs of Ireland: Harp Lager. Tilt and bows helped protect the beer from the elements.

Looking as if it's seen some hard service and in need of a clean, this Transporter delivered brown sauce for a living.

Barcastle's sausage delivery van looks like it's carrying quite a load, judging from the way the front wheels are tucked up in the wheel arches!

J J Byrne Ltd also liked to use pick-ups for deliveries. Note the slogan on the front panel: 'This is THE Place'.

The General Electric Company of Ireland Ltd used both Transporters and pick-ups in the line of duty. Large spotlight on the front bumper made up for weak 6-volt headlamps.

To cut down on commuting costs on business trips to Washington DC, in 1964 this group of advertising executives from New York clubbed together to rent a Microbus!

In the USA, the Dick Mitchell Electric company ran a fleet of seven Transporters back in the late '50s, along with sundry Chevrolets and other domestic vehicles.

The 'Recruitmobile' was a 23-window Samba used by the US Navy recruiting team in Des Moines, Iowa, back in 1960. It served as a mobile information centre and appeared regularly in local parades.

The League of Women Voters borrowed a fleet of 13 Sambas to help encourage women across America to register so that they could vote in the 1964 Presidential campaign.

In 1961, 'The Chargers' football team purchased two Transporters for use as mobile ticket offices, following the team's move from Los Angeles down to San Diego in southern California. The vehicles proved to be a big hit with fans.

The Deutsche Bundespost was a loyal customer. Row upon row of Transporters and crew-cab pick-ups are seen awaiting delivery to the Bundespost in 1964, while the 1953 photo below shows a new Transporter ready for delivery, complete with special security lock on the side door.

Taken at Hamburg airport in 1953, this photo shows an interesting line-up of vehicles, including a trio of early Sambas and a couple of special high-roof conversions.

A trio of airport workhorses, consisting of a 1952 British European Airways Kombi, a 1953 petrol delivery truck and a 1952 Coca-Cola van. Note the fixed roof rack on the BEA vehicle.

This Samba was built very early in 1953 (no rear bumper – just rubbing strips attached to body) and was used at Hamburg airport as a shuttle bus. Full Samba trim included chrome dress rings on the wheels.

This 1954 pick-up was also used by the USAF as a crash tender. Signs appear to be only temporary, secured by clips at each corner.

This 1953 or '54 Kombi (right) was used by the Police department of the USAF in Germany. It was equipped with a rear bumper, only available to special order at this time. Note roof fresh air vent.

Coca-Cola delivery Transporter dates back to late 1950 or early 1951. Colours were red over yellow.

Westfalia Kombi was in use by ADAC — the German road safety organisation. The low-level body trim is an interesting feature. Rear wheels are non-standard on this example.

At first glance this looks like any other delivery van (above and right), but the small vent high up at the rear of the vehicle suggests otherwise. It's an ice-cream delivery van, with a second set of insulated doors inside the regular side doors. Vent at rear is for on-board refrigerator.

Unusual colour scheme gives a whole new look to the wheel arch shape of this late-1951 Transporter (used, incidentally, for delivering cheese and fat). Note the tiny VW badge on the nose – presumably taken from a Beetle.

Michael Steinke's 1966 Samba, complete with original whitewall tyres, is often used as a wedding vehicle and is especially attractive in its red and white colour scheme.

Samba, the guard dog, looks after Michael's late-'66 Westfalia. Who needs an alarm system?

A 1972 Deluxe Microbus with optional bumper and side trim, chromed mirrors and front badge. Building is decorated in the traditional German country style.

This unusual test, being carried out on a 1977 Transporter, was to ensure that no liquids (fuel, oil, etc) could spill out in the event of a roll-over accident.

Horse-drawn 'taxi' consisted of the cab from a Kombi. The rest of the vehicle was used to make a second horse-drawn taxi! This was one environmentally friendly idea that, fortunately, didn't catch on.

Jupp, the dummy ambulance man, looks after the only known surviving original ambulance and trailer 'train', seen here at the Bad Camberg vintage meeting in 1995.

If dummy ambulance men are not your scene, how about a few dummy policemen from around the world! Crazy VW publicity photo was intended to suggest that the VW bus could be used by police forces throughout the world.

Volkswagen obviously had something about dummies...

These dummies had nothing to smile about – they played a vital role during crash-testing the Type 2 for the American market.

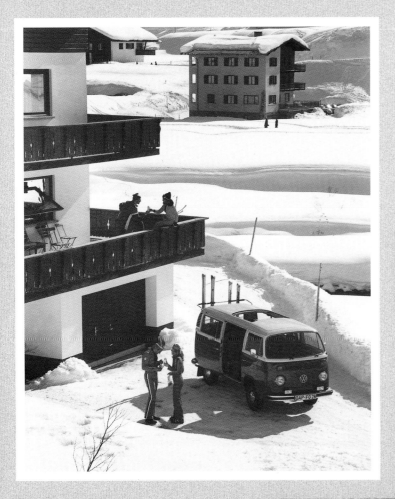

With its rear-mounted engine and drivetrain, even a Westfalia 'Joker' can cope with most winter situations, such as these in the Italian Dolomites.

How about a skiing holiday in Austria, just you, your friends and a '76 Bus?

Of course, when the going gets really tough, there's no substitute for a Syncro with snow plough attachment! 'Unstoppable' is the word that comes to mind.

The Syncro really excels in snow, this single-cab pick-up making light work of a snow-covered forestry track.

You don't have to drive a dune buggy to enjoy the sand dunes of Glamis in southern California — an all-wheel drive Syncro will do just as well.

Desert, warm sunshine, blue skies, cacti and an air-conditioned VR6 Eurovan — Arizona 1998.

'Oscar the Talking Police Car' was built by Police in Canada as part of a road safety education programme aimed at young children. Say 'Hello!' to Oscar...

Of course, there are always going to be people who can't leave their buses alone, like the owner of this German-registered vehicle seen on the cover of a 1959 edition of Gute Fahrt Junior. Weight of badges must have knocked 10mph off the top speed...

Halt! Erratet einmal blitzschnell, wieviel Plaketten an diesem VW-Bus angeschraubt sind! 20 – 30 – 100 – oder wie viele? Ihr könnt auch eure Freunde raten lassen und damit testen, ob sie gut zu schätzen vermögen. – Der VW-Bus hat übrigens – wie man sieht – gerade eine Reise um die halbe Welt hinter sich.

Very attractive Samba and matching trailer combination from the USA. Trailer is built from the rear half of a single-cab pick-up and then fitted with a tonneau cover.

Very strange one-off conversion on a Samba featured raised cab area, with specially extended door tops and panoramic roof lights.

Steam power? No, just another publicity vehicle – this time for a hotel. Beneath the disguise, it's a crew-cab pick-up from the mid-'70s.

At first, this is hard to identify. It's a special crew-cab conversion by Stahl in Germany, complete with a unique body kit which totally disguises the third-generation Transporter beneath. Flat rear bed is to allow hook-up of a 'fifth wheel' trailer unit.

The 1973 'Muli' was a simple vehicle supplied in CKD (completely knocked down) form to Third World markets. It featured a conventional chassis with a front-mounted Beetle engine and gearbox driving the front wheels through a combination of VW K70 parts. It was designed by Gustav Mayer, the man responsible for both the second- and third-generation Transporters. Just 3194 of these vehicles were produced by VW's Mexican factory.

To celebrate the 40th year of the Transporter, VW showed this T4 van complete with a suitably retrospective design on the side.

A roadside chapel, or something altogether more intriguing? Look closely and you'll see that the 'tower' is made from the rear of a VW bus!

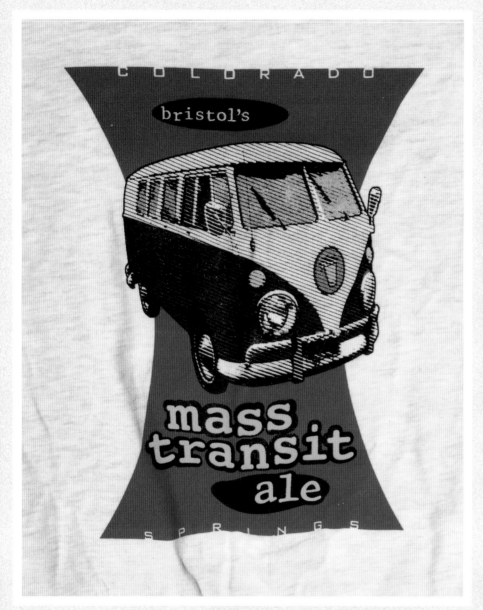

Across the world, the VW bus has become a symbol of freedom and individuality. Its image appears on everything from advertising material to clothing.

Just when you think you've seen it all, along come these sunglasses for the truly extrovert bus addict!

Hand-painted tiles depicting your Samba? Why not!

Buses get everywhere! In the USA, you can even buy a mail box in the form of a Samba.

Old VW buses never die — they just spend their last days rusting peacefully among the trees of Ohio.

Westfalia camper has seen better days but, who knows, someone may come to the rescue before it crumbles to dust.

Look closely and you'll discover that this used to be a 23-window Samba! Most of the roof windows and the sun-roof have been filled, but at least one window is left and you can still see where the side trim went.

The VW bus as art. This is, officially, the world's most expensive VW. It forms part of a 'sculpture' by the artist Joseph Beuys. In the '70s it was estimated to be worth DM 1.5 million, but in 1993 it sold for a heart-stopping DM 16.5 million (or about £6 million or just under $10 million)! The title is 'Das Rudel' — 'The Pack'. Now you have seen it all...

Happy new owner takes delivery of his latest restoration 'project' – a rare 1961 ladder truck.

Extreme nose-down attitude suggests hard braking but wheels have not locked, even on a wet surface, because this bus is equipped with experimental ABS – anti-lock braking.

Don't look now, something's following you! Chequered Transporter is a modern 'Follow Me' bus in use at Hannover airport for escorting aircraft along the taxiway.

Name your colour, name your model! First-generation buses of all types gather at a German show.

EPIC ADVENTURES
Transporters take on the world

It's difficult to know quite what constitutes an epic journey for a Volkswagen, for what would have been a marathon for most other vehicles is all in a day's work for the Transporter. It's not uncommon, for example, for groups of Australian students to buy VW campers in Sydney and then drive them halfway round the world to London in search of work and a new social life.

Invariably these campers are well-used, frequently abused and definitely a far cry from the concours examples found at most VW shows. However, with some care and attention and occasionally a little good luck, they will usually provide trouble-free transport, coping with the worst terrain thanks to their rugged construction and almost unbreakable suspension. Even when things do go wrong, there's usually somebody nearby who can fix a VW, and spares are available world-wide.

There have been some truly amazing journeys completed in a Volkswagen Type 2, one of the first – if not the first – being that undertaken in 1950 by a team of Belgians led by Pierre D'Ieteren. This arduous 25,000km adventure through Africa saw the team drive their 1950

Above: Trans Amazonas adventure in the '70s saw a group of Type 2s tackling seemingly impenetrable scenery. Mud, mud and more mud made it an arduous journey.

Kombi, and a VW Beetle of similar vintage, to the Belgian Congo and back. For three months they endured some truly atrocious conditions, ranging from soft sand and scorching heat to glutinous mud and torrential rain. The Volkswagens took it all in their stride...

Many VWs have made the trip all the way round the world, one example being the camper of the Mottiez family from Switzerland who, in 1960, decided to circumnavigate the globe via five continents. By the time they arrived in the USA, where the family was treated like royalty, they had already covered 115,000 trouble-free miles. The trip, referred to by VW of America as 'Around the world in 800 days' was completed without mishap.

Today, there still exists a spirit of adventure among Volkswagen enthusiasts across the world and there's no better example of this than the trips undertaken by the Bulli Kartei club in Germany. Under the leadership of Michael

Steinke, in 1992 the club decided to organise a humanitarian convoy to Sarajevo, Bosnia, using a variety of largely Split-screen Transporters of every description. Having collected literally tons of clothes, shoes, sweets and toys, the convoy set off but had to divert via Hungary into Romania due to the war that was still taking place in Bosnia. The 'target' was the CARITAS aid programme, in the city of Satu Mare, where the convoy was welcomed with open arms.

Since that first trip, members of Bulli Kartei and friends have repeated the exercise no fewer than 12 times, to the delight of the beneficiaries. In addition to the food and clothing supplies, by 1998 the convoys had delivered a total of nine VW cars, four VW single-cab pick-ups, four vans, four ambulances and a small trailer, all of which had been donated either by club members, the Automuseum Wolfsburg, the citizens of Frankfurt or a number of local businesses, including VW dealers like W. Lottermann of Bad Camberg. These humanitarian trips were run under the title of 'Bullis bringen Freude', or 'Transporters bring joy', 'Bulli' being the German nickname for the trusty VW commercial.

Although not the longest journey ever completed in a VW bus, the epic 25,000km tour through Africa undertaken in 1950 by Pierre D'Ieteren, Christian Nicolaï de Gorhez, Jacques Cortvriendt and Jacques Swaters was probably one of the most arduous. The team of four set off in a VW Beetle and a Kombi. Their tale is told in this book, written by D'Ieteren and de Gorhez.

When all else failed, the only option was to manhandle the Volkswagens out of the mud. Fortunately, there always seemed to be plenty of willing hands ready to help out.

Photo shows the bus being unloaded at Algiers. This was long before the days of roll-on/roll-off car ferries and even a relatively simple operation like this was fraught with danger.

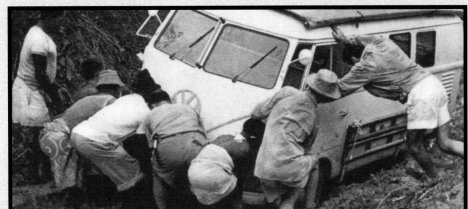

Conditions in parts of Africa were terrible, heavy rains having turned what were usually passable roads into a quagmire. Much effort was spent digging out the vehicles. Note the rare cool-air vent in the cab door.

The route took the team down into Central Africa, to an area known then as the Belgian Congo. Along the way, they met many of the local tribesmen, most of whom were fascinated by the antics of these hardy Belgians.

This Westfalia, complete with trademark roof racks (two of them in tandem!), ventured into Africa in 1961 where it, too, was greeted with great interest by local tribesmen.

A short break in a lava field in North Africa for this well-equipped Bay-window camper on its way to the Sahara desert.

In 1960, Louis Mottiez, an engineer from Lausanne in Switzerland, decided to drive his camper round the world, visiting VW dealerships along the way. In company with wife Milly and son Claude, Mottiez had covered some 115,000 miles by the time he arrived in the USA, his route having taken him through Europe, Asia, Australia and South, Central and North America. A story in VW of America's magazine, Weathervane, was entitled 'Around the world in 800 days'.

Sand and more sand! It can take several hours to dig a vehicle out of soft sand, only for it to become embedded again a few yards later. Aluminium runners have to be used under the tyres to give the necessary help with grip.

In 1992 members of the German Bulli-Kartei (VW bus club) organised a humanitarian aid trip that ended in the city of Satu Mare, Romania. The aim was to take vital provisions to this former eastern-bloc country in a convoy of Type 2s of all descriptions, including former fire trucks and ambulances. A variety of split-screen emergency vehicles take well-earned rests in the two shots above.

On the way to Mostar, Bosnia, in 1995 – the ambulance was to be donated to the people of Mostar. The Westfalia ambulance trailer contained 10 folding wheelchairs donated to the cause.

The 'Bullis' have visited Bosnia or Romania every year since 1992, with other trips planned for the future. This is part of the 1998 line-up, including a Split-screen pick-up, Arcomobil camper, van and high-roof fire truck en route to Romania.

On its way to the North Cape, the Steinke family's '71 Westfalia prepares to board the car ferry Aallotar in Stockholm.

Northward bound! The road sign reads 'Drive Slowly'. Looking at the road surface, that was sound advice!

In 1985, two British policemen — Paul Radzan and Clive Shonard — entered the gruelling 'Cop Drive', a two-day off-road driving competition held in Britain between members of the Army and the Police. They chose to drive a relatively standard VW Syncro, powered by a 1.9-litre petrol engine, which, needless to say, never let them down.

On 2 January 1985, Rudi Lins and Gerhard Plattner left Innsbruck, Austria, on a round-the-world record attempt in a Syncro. They covered a total of 46,000km, arriving home after just 129 days on 15 May.

The route took them through 34 countries in five continents and was completed without major mishap, other than rolling the vehicle and hitting a kangaroo in Australia!

Volkswagen builds 'em tough! This highly modified all-wheel-drive LT was built to tackle the famous Paris-Dakar rally in 1982, acting as a support vehicle to the Yamaha motorcycle team.

A factory-supported Syncro crew-cab tackled the Hannibal Rally in 1985, an event which retraced the route taken by Hannibal while crossing the Alps with his elephants.

INDEX